SUCCESS
AND SURVIVAL
ON
WALL STREET

SUCCESS AND SURVIVAL ON WALL STREET

Understanding the Mind of the Market

Charles W. Smith

ROWMAN & LITTLEFIELD PUBLISHERS, INC.
Lanham • Boulder • New York • Oxford

ROWMAN & LITTLEFIELD PUBLISHERS, INC.

Published in the United States of America
by Rowman & Littlefield Publishers, Inc.
4720 Boston Way, Lanham, Maryland 20706
http://www.rowmanlittlefield.com

12 Hid's Copse Road
Cumnor Hill, Oxford OX2 9JJ, England

British Library Cataloguing in Publication Information Available

Library of Congress Cataloging-in-Publication Data

Smith, Charles W., 1938–
    Success and survival on Wall Street : understanding the mind of
the market / Charles W. Smith.
      p. cm.
    Includes bibliographical references and index.
    ISBN 0-8476-9490-9 (cl. : alk. paper)
    1. Investments—United States.   2. Stock exchanges—United States.
I. Title.
HG4910.S5634   1999
332.6—dc21   99-25945
                                             CIP

Printed in the United States of America

♾ ™ The paper used in this publication meets the minimum requirements of
American National Standard for Information Sciences—Permanence of Paper
for Printed Library Materials, ANSI Z39.48–1992.

CONTENTS

PREFACE

This book is concerned with the ways in which values are assigned to financial instruments—primarily stocks—on Wall Street. More broadly, like its predecessor—*The Mind of the Market*—this book is also concerned with the ways the market is viewed, interpreted, and evaluated. It is not intended as a "how to make money" book nor as an organizational study of the stock market, though at times it sheds light on both subjects.

Like its predecessor, this book was long in the making. Over the years I have continually been urged by friends and colleagues to do a sequel to, or minimally revise, *The Mind of the Market*. I had always hesitated to do so, though, because I really didn't feel that I had that much more to add to what I had already written. The dramatic changes occurring in the market over the last few years, however—the unprecedented advance in prices, the growth in volume, increased public awareness, the introduction of new technology, changing exchange structure—caused me to begin to question my position.

More recently, my resolve was further tested by my son, who—having some spare time between medical school and his first hospital appointment—decided to read his father's *old* stock market book. To both his and my surprise, he found it most interesting and useful. His advice to me was both direct and simple: "Hey Dad, you should definitely update this book. I know that a lot of my friends would really benefit from it. Most of them don't know how to make any sense out of all the rhetoric they hear."

As with the first book, I have tried to make my story accessible to all by minimizing the use of market jargon while still maintaining an accurate "feel" of the market by including a glossary of stock market terminology, which those unfamiliar with such jargon should find useful. I have also tried to avoid going off on various "practical advice" tangents by packaging what advice I have to give in a final section entitled "Some Practical Advice for the Individual Investor." Finally, to make the study as accessible as possible to nonsociologists, I have tried wherever possible to present my more theoretical observations implicitly within the narrative context; in the first and last chapters, however, I have addressed some of these issues directly. I have also included a brief theoretical and methodological note.

Although the market has changed in a number of respects since I wrote my previous book—visibility, technology, size, etc.—it remains basically the same when it comes to how it is viewed, interpreted, and evaluated, and in its basic investment strategies. For this reason, I have elected to use a good deal of the material from the earlier book as a platform for this account. I have also elected to structure this book in the same way the first book was structured. It begins by presenting a general overview of the various ways the market is commonly perceived, emphasizing the degree to which most people see the market as ambiguous and confusing. Whereas twenty years ago the market was framed in terms of four dominant perspectives—the Fundamentalist, Insider, Chartist-Cyclist, and Trader frameworks—today it tends to be framed in terms of six frameworks: the four just noted, which still dominate, and what are called the Efficient Market framework and the Transformational Idea framework.

Part 2 presents ideal prototypes for each of these dominant positions that are based upon the many real people I have interviewed over the years. I call them my True Believers, since unlike most market players, they truly believe that they understand how the market works.

Part 3 takes these overviews and describes the various ways they are used by salespersons and others to sell the market. Again, I make use of ideal prototypes based upon the many real people I have met over nearly forty years.

Because so much time has passed since I began this research, I have elected where possible to present my prototypes over time, starting with how they saw the market twenty years ago and how their views have since changed. In doing so, I have obviously used statements of observations from different individuals, but I have attempted to remain loyal to the specific types. This technique allows us to get a good feel not only for where we are today but also for where we have been.

Part 4 takes a step back from the various styles in which the market is interpreted to focus more on how the market is experienced. Here I look at the way cynicism, faith, and foolishness shape the way some participants respond to the market. Although the unprecedented price rise of the market in recent years has diminished the visibility of market cynics, their views still pervade the market, albeit in a more shadowy form. Conversely, this rise has given new impetus to a form of broad optimism and almost-blind faith in the market that has not been this strong since before the crash of 1929. This emphasis upon the role that emotions can and do play in the market made it sensible to expand my earlier discussion of crowd behavior and to include it in this section. This section, chapter 15, also contains an analysis of computer program trading, which for all practical purposes did not exist twenty years ago.

In Part 5, I put it all together. The greater visibility that the market has had in recent years dramatically affects the market's influence on all segments of society—and vice versa. Not only is the market sensitive to what goes on everywhere, but also the world as a whole is in turn sensitive to what happens in the market. This mutuality is evident nowhere more dramatically than in the manner in which people think and frame issues. To use Robert K. Merton's phrase, the market has become a, if not the, premier strategic research site for doing the sociology of knowledge.[1] Part 5 explores some of these issues.

Part 6, as noted above, offers some practical advice to the individual investor based on the analysis and discussion that precede it.

I remain deeply indebted to the many people who work on Wall Street who assisted me in producing my earlier book, as well as those who assisted me in this new endeavor. Unfortunately, nearly all of these market professionals, by agreement, must remain anonymous. They know who they are, and I hope and trust that they will be pleased by their efforts and contributions.

I am also indebted to numerous colleagues. Twenty years ago when I wrote the precursor to this volume, few sociologists shared my interest in the stock market. During the last decade, however, a growing number of sociologists have turned toward economic sociology and the market, and I have benefited greatly from their intellectual and emotive support. I am particularly grateful to those who participated with me in the Russell Sage Foundation seminar in Economic Sociology in 1990–1991, and to those from the Society for the Advancement of Economic Sociology (SASE) and the emerging American Sociological Association's section in Economic Sociology. Two colleagues, Karin Knoor Cetina and Viviana Zelizer, deserve special thanks.

Special thanks are also due to Dean Birkenkamp of Rowman & Littlefield, who not only urged me to undertake this project, but who has been an invaluable support throughout the process, and Scott Horst and his team for their editorial assistance. I want also to publicly thank my wife, Rita, daughter, Abigail, and son, Jonathan, for continuing to listen; and Gerald D. Weintraub, who for over forty years has served not only as my market alter ego but also as a constant mentor and good friend.

   I would like to end this brief preface by noting, as I did in the first book, that it is not my intention in stressing the *mind of the market* to deny that there are stocks, stock exchanges, stock transactions, rules, and regulations that have an existence of their own. There is, of course, the market described by the pamphlets put out by the New York Stock Exchange. But these pamphlets describe only the skin and bones of the market; they do not describe the less tangible elements that give life to the market. It is one of the major objectives of this book to explore these elements and in so doing to make sense of the market as it is actually experienced and as it actually functions. In keeping with this objective, I will begin again with the market as it is most often seen— namely, as confused, confusing, enigmatic, and paradoxical.

                                                        C. W. S.

PART I

THE AMBIGUITY OF THE MARKET

1

WHAT'S GOING ON?

Seventeen years ago I began by noting, "The only thing clear about the market is that nothing is clear. The market is variously defined, and the same event may have completely different meanings for different persons." In this respect, the market hasn't changed much over the years. This doesn't mean that the market hasn't changed in other ways. During the last few decades all sorts of things have happened.

During the last decade of the millennium perhaps the most noticeable change has been the sharp rise in the market. Most major indexes reflect nearly a tenfold increase during this period. Perhaps more dramatic have been the threefold gains from the early nineties to the 1999 highs. This rise in price has been accompanied by an even more dramatic rise in volume and visibility. In 1980, a twenty-million-share day on the New York Stock Exchange was a busy day. Today, daily trading on the New York Stock Exchange is measured in the high hundreds of millions, with approximately the same number of shares being traded on the NASDAQ.[2]

In the late seventies, the New York Stock Exchange dominated the market, being the place where the stocks of most major companies were traded. Today the NASDAQ competes on an equal footing and is the home for the majority of high-technology companies including Microsoft, Intel, Cisco, and Dell. The growth of technology is also reflected in the way Wall Street does its business. More and more transactions are done by computer. More and more services are provided online. This has given rise to a whole new group of discount trading firms and online service providers. At the same time, the number of older firms has declined due to this competition and to mergers.

The growth in the market and the rise in equity prices have drawn many more people into the market. The number of individual investors has grown from approximately thirty million to well over fifty million. There has been an even more dramatic, hundredfold growth in the number of mutual funds. There has also been an expansion in the types of products offered for sale, including a whole range of what are referred to as derivatives: futures, options, and the like.

However else these factors have influenced the market—we will examine all of them more closely in coming chapters—they clearly haven't made things any clearer. In fact, they have probably served to make things more confusing. Most investors are still likely to have had experiences similar to those in the following dramatization.

Eleven fifteen in the morning—the telephone of our investor rings. His broker wants him to buy a few hundred shares of a stock that she[3] has been following. The earnings[4] of the company, she tells him, have just come across the ticker and they are up; she thinks the stock is good for a quick 20 percent move. "Okay," the customer says, "buy two hundred shares."

Three days later, he gives his broker a call. He wants to know how his stocks are doing, especially the new one he just bought. His broker tells him that so far nothing much has happened. She is glad he called, however, because she has another situation for him. Another stock that she has been following has just come out with its earnings and they were down. The stock has sold off a few points and she thinks that it is ripe for buying. It could sell off some more, but she thinks it is time to start nibbling at it. She wants him to buy a hundred shares. She's the expert, our investor tells himself, so he allows his broker to buy a hundred shares at the current market.

Two weeks later he is having lunch with his brother-in-law; they begin to talk about the market. The brother-in-law notes that his broker has been pushing him to buy a particular company that is rumored to have an exciting new product. Our customer gets quite excited, because he already owns some shares in the company. That afternoon he calls his broker to see if she thinks that more shares should be bought based on his brother-in-law's rumor. To his surprise, his broker tells him that it would be a good time to sell what he already owns. "You'd be better off putting your money in GHP; it's rumored that ZYX is trying to take them over."

Two days later our friend logs on to a chart service to which he has taken a trial membership. The service is very bearish. It argues that many stocks are trading in the upper ranges of their normal trading ranges. It strongly recommends selling a significant portion of one's holdings. That same day on the train to work, a neighbor informs him that she is seriously considering taking the recommendation of another chart service, which argues that the market is ready to break out of its old trading range and make new highs for the year. Later that morning our customer calls his broker to get her feelings; his broker tells him that she feels that all of the chart services are not worth the paper they are printed on or the space they take up on the Web.

As he hangs up the telephone, a feeling of confusion sets in. He asks himself if he's crazy or just stupid. He concludes that if he is going to play the market, he better give the market a little more time, since the way things are now, he doesn't understand what's going on. Starting tomorrow, he will carefully read the financial section of his paper; he will even read the *Wall Street Journal*. He'll also sign up for a few more services that he can get on the Web. He figures he'll try one that focuses on earnings and underlying value and another that focuses on technical data.

The next morning, after checking the prices of his stocks, he reads a long article based upon an in-depth interview with one of the most successful money managers on Wall Street. It's a little difficult to follow all of the arguments, but one thing is perfectly clear: The expert is very bullish. Equally important, our friend feels that he is finally reaching those individuals who know what makes the market tick. Unfortunately, the next day, while logged on to one of his Internet services, he comes upon another article based upon an interview with another market expert who is just as bearish as the first was bullish. When our friend's broker calls that afternoon, he tells his secretary to tell the broker that he is tied up and that he will get back to her later. For the rest of the week, he doesn't even look at the financial pages.

Friday evening, he decides to give it another try. With a double scotch he settles down in front of his television to watch *Wall Street Week*. There are three panelists and a guest speaker, all highly respected market professionals.

Again, there is widespread disagreement, but no one seems to be bothered by it; one would almost think, the way they smile and nod at each other's statements, that they were in agreement. Moreover, whenever it is pointed out that what they said a few weeks ago proved incorrect, they are ready with an explanation that makes it sound as if they had, in fact, been correct. In short, they don't seem to be confused.

As the show ends, our friend is totally muddled. One day he is told to buy a stock because the earnings are up; the next day he is told to buy another stock because the earnings are down. He is told to sell in response to one good rumor and to buy in response to another good rumor. Some people say that he should sell when stocks are up and others tell him to buy. As far as he can determine, it doesn't make any sense, but then there are all these professionals to whom it apparently does makes sense. He sits there asking himself which of them is right. Are any of them right? Pulling himself together, he proceeds to his home office and logs on to the Website of a market service to which he subscribes. Within a few minutes he is surfing the Web, reading market-advice columns prominently displayed on various sites. Here again he finds the same things, namely a hodgepodge of contradictory advice. What is one to make of it all?

The most obvious conclusion to draw from our investor's dilemma is that he is an amateur and as such doesn't have the faintest idea about what is going on. However, when we turn to the professionals—the stockbrokers, money managers, analysts, and their sort—we find that they are apt to see the market as just as ambiguous and as confusing as does our amateur friend.[5] If anything, professionals tend to be more conflicted, because in addition to trying to understand the market, they must, in one form or another, sell their expertise. Though they seldom admit their uncertainties in public, their uncertainties clearly emerged in the course of my interviews. Most of the supposedly more sophisticated professionals I talked with twenty-five years ago weren't sure what the market was, what it was supposed to be, or what it wanted to be. Since they said it all, I will let them speak for themselves. Since I guaranteed that their names would not be used, however, they cannot be identified; I have consequently used pseudonyms. All statements attributed, however, are real.[6]

Harry Silver was a senior partner in a large, primarily institutional, brokerage house. As such he had direct access to one of the most prestigious research departments on Wall Street. What did he think of the market? "It's a crap game." What about all the research that his firm puts out? "It helps sell stocks, but it isn't worth the paper it is written on."

Are there any people in the market who know what is going on? "There are a few, but most of them can't make a living; they either don't know how, or are unwilling, to play the game."

How then do you select the people you put into the more sensitive positions? How do you decide whether a broker is put into retail sales or is moved into institutional sales, where he is expected to be more sophisticated? "Usually by the school he went to and his social class."

How does all this affect you? "I wait for the day I can retire." Do you invest your own money? "Yes." What approach do you use? "I follow the guy in the office who has the hottest hand. I'm the public. I want action."

Doesn't this whole situation bother you? "Only when I think about it."

Jack Reed was a money manager; he ran portfolios whose values were in excess of four hundred million dollars, which would be worth over a billion dollars today. What did he think about the market? "Basically a 'no win' situation." How did he cope with such a situation? "By trying to maintain a balanced, diversified position with a fair amount of assets in bonds." Would he ever consider structuring his portfolios as a quasi-index fund? "Yes, but I would never admit that is what I had done. If I did, I would be out of a job."[7]

Did he think it possible to manage money according to his own best market judgment? "Yes, but the risks are too great; if you are wrong, you are likely to lose the account. It is much safer to give your client pretty much what he wants and what he is likely to get anywhere else. Then, if things go badly, at least you are in good company."

In light of all this, how did he see the market? What is it? "It is the WPA of the upper classes. It is a place where you can put junior to work and assure him a good living—providing you have the contacts—without having to worry that he is going to screw up the economy or the government. It is a much better system than they have in England, where they put him to work in an important position and where he can do real damage."

Did he ever think about getting out of the market? "All the time. Unfortunately, I doubt that I could make the same living doing anything else. Perhaps the one thing I think about doing most is to buy a seat on one of the smaller exchanges and then just to trade for myself."

In many ways, Harry Silver and Jack Reed took opposite positions on the market. Harry Silver was primarily critical of those who thought that they understood the market; Jack Reed was more critical of those only interested in sales. Still, they agreed on many points. Both had a highly critical view of most market professionals. The only difference they saw between an institutional broker and a retail broker was that the former had a more polished self-presentation. Both also believed that the market was pretty much a hoax. Both, however, retained a very real fondness for the market. Others took an even more critical view; Ben Decker was one such person.

Ben Decker pulled no punches; he didn't have to. He was eminently successful. Among the numerous companies in which he had a controlling interest was a brokerage firm. He had been around the market for more than twenty years and knew it inside and out. What did he think of the market? "It's a sham."

To hear a man thought by many to be a Wall Street wizard state that the market is a sham is, to say the least, a little disconcerting. I felt that he was kidding me. It would be one thing to point out the flaws of the market, but to publicly state, not just imply, that the whole market is a fraud is something else. It didn't take me long to realize that he was deadly serious.

Why did he believe the market is a sham? "Because all theories about how to beat the market are based upon the assumption that there is some body of knowledge which is capable of explaining the market, but such a body of knowledge simply does not exist. The market is too complex. People who think that they understand the market are fooling themselves. There are no exceptions. In fact, those who think they understand the market best—for instance, money managers, institutional types, and market analysts—are generally the biggest fools of all. Most people, at least, know that they don't understand what is going on."

If he truly believed this, how could he buy stocks? He claimed he didn't and hadn't bought a stock for years; he bought companies. "Stocks are for the public and people who have nothing better to do with their money." Here he distinguished between someone who buys a 20 percent interest in a company and thereby acquires a controlling interest from those who merely invest in stocks. "The market offers great opportunities for the first type because there is no logic to the market; there are plenty of undervalued situations. The latter approach is only for those who have nothing better to do with their money. The market may be a great place for someone to learn about the way our economy and political system works. It is also a place where someone can find excitement. It is definitely not a place to make money."[8]

This attitude colored Ben Decker's view of those involved in the market. "No one knows anything. The only difference between the more prestigious firms and the less prestigious is the amount of veneer. Most prestigious firms are also less likely to try to screw you." He was quick to add that anyone who had been around Wall Street for any length of time knew this. "Why do you think that every RR wants to be something else? They only stick with it because they can't make as much money doing anything else. By and large they're lazy and ignorant. Most of them earn ten times what they could earn doing anything else. If you figure it in terms of the hours they put in, the ratio would be more like fifty times what they could earn doing another job."

If this is the way he felt, why did he own a brokerage firm? "Because it is a great business. Where else can you make as much money with such a small investment?"

As I said earlier, Ben Decker doesn't pull his punches, though actually he overstates his case. After an hour of listening to him debunk the market, I began to push a little. I told him that I really didn't believe that no one could beat the market. I felt that he could beat the market and that he knew it. Pushed, he admitted that, if he had no alternative, he could make money in the market following a very strict fundamentalist approach. "This doesn't contradict what I have been saying, because if I had the financial resources to invest, I would still be much better off buying companies rather than stocks. Furthermore, if I had to make my living as a broker, I would never be able to generate enough commissions."

I asked him if it would be possible if he had a number of very large accounts. He countered by saying that it would never work. "To maintain large accounts, one must be able to project an image of success, and that requires a large income. The commission structure, especially with discounts, doesn't generate such incomes unless one is willing to do some churning. To maintain accounts worth $25,000,000, for example [remember, he is talking in 1980], a broker must come across as at least a couple of hundred thousand dollars-a-year man; to maintain $10,000,000 worth of accounts, he must come across as someone earning $100,000 a year. Without churning, the first guy would be lucky to earn $70,000, and the second guy $35,000. On the other hand, if they do churn, then they will no longer be functioning as true fundamentalists. In short, a broker without money of his own would starve if he tried to operate as a true Fundamentalist."[9]

He added, "Brokerage firms find themselves in a similar situation. A brokerage firm can't afford to be bearish. They'd go broke. They have to be able to recommend stocks for purchase." Couldn't they do business if they followed a technical approach? "That's the absolute height of tomfoolery. The technicians are the high priests of sham; that's witchcraft."

Despite Ben Decker's cynical views, I felt that on one level the market made sense to him. Here I was looking for something analogous to Harry Silver's view that the market was one giant crap game or to Jack Reed's view that the market was the WPA of the upper classes. Ben Decker did have such a vision, and it was clearly a more eccentric one.

What had Ben Decker concluded after his many years in the market? What basic order did the market reflect? "Heterosexuals tend to buy stocks, homosexuals bonds; convertible bond buyers tend to be bisexual, and short sellers tend to be the true 'machos' of the market." He was quite serious about this. "It all has to do with the degree of security one wants in a relationship. The safe relationship is the homosexual relationship; bonds are the safe investment, etc." He added that he would find a study that dealt with this aspect of the market very interesting.

In concluding our discussion, Ben Decker added that in many ways the market was the height of self-deception. "It is a bunch of people who are trying to fool themselves intellectually. This requires that they attempt to fool others." I asked him if it didn't bother him when he was the object of such attempts. He smiled and answered. "No. I don't take the sham of the market personally."

Norman Walters took the sham of the market very personally. By and large he shared the negative view of the market that Harry Silver, Jack Reed, and Ben Decker held. There was one major difference. Norman Walters believed that there was an order to the market and that the market could be mastered. To him, it was not just a question of ignorance; it was also a moral question.

Norman Walters was one of the premier money managers of Wall Street. Many ran more money then he, but few, if any, had a better reputation. Basically, he was a Fundamentalist, though he had incorporated elements from other approaches. Where he differed most from the average money managers was in his cosmopolitan view of the market. He was very concerned with world trends and the general sociopolitical environment. In short, he was committed to a broad view of the market and judged the market in terms of this broad view. What had he concluded?

"The market has lost its meaning to most who make their living in it and from it. One can contrast most American market professionals with their Swiss counterparts. I'm not sure that the Swiss experts on average do any better for their clients than the American experts do. There is, however, one major difference. The Swiss see themselves as having a sacred trust. They see themselves as the defenders of their clients' economic freedom. As such, they take great pride in what they're trying to do. They may not always be successful, but they don't doubt their own intentions or objectives. The Americans, in contrast, don't feel this way. The pressures upon them to sell stocks and to perform have made most of them very cynical. In many ways they are too sophisticated. They always have to project an image of themselves as knowledgeable. Most know that it is a false image. As a result, they have lost their self-respect. Many have come to see themselves as highly paid con men. In most cases, they have even less respect for their colleagues. They don't see themselves as doing anything meaningful or useful. As a result, they are unable to take seriously the very real responsibilities they have. Whatever their intellectual limitations might be have been compounded by this loss of purpose. As a consequence, they perform more poorly than their limited knowledge itself would dictate. They continue to go through the motions, but most have simply given up."

Although all professionals twenty years ago didn't see the market as futile and meaningless as those just quoted, it was more the general view than the public realized. The situation has changed somewhat in recent years due primarily to the unprecedented rise in prices during the last decade. Whereas the Dow Jones Industrial Average kept within an approximate range of 600 to 1000 from 1963 through 1982, it broke the 2000 mark in early 1987, the 3000 mark in 1990, the 4000 mark in 1994, 5000 in 1995, 6000 in 1996, 8000 in 1997, 9000 in early 1998, 10,000 and then 11,000 in 1999. Not surprisingly, this has caused many professional and lay investors alike to believe that the only sensible investment strategy is to be fully invested in the market.[10] Although most professionals aren't that optimistic, most are considerably more positive today than was the case twenty years ago. It should be noted, however, that many are considerably less optimistic in private than they are in public.

Michael Vacco is probably among the more truly committed optimists on today's Wall Street. He came to Wall Street after completing two tours in the Marines in Vietnam, where he distinguished himself. He has worked for three different firms during his twenty-five years on the street and presently occupies a top management position in one of Wall Street's larger firms. Mike is gung ho on the American stock market. Though many, if not most, of the market professionals who have been around since the sixties clearly worry about the exuberance of the market during the nineties, Mike argues that the best is yet to come. "Where else can you put your money for the long haul? Okay, it makes sense to put some of your resources in bonds, but the real play over time is the market. With an aging population, pension funds and mutual funds are just going to keep on growing, and as long as that money keeps coming in the market will keep going up. Some of the money will probably find a home abroad in other markets, but the American market still dwarfs all the other markets combined. There simply is nowhere else to go."

The fact that one elects to be fully, or even just heavily, invested in the market because one expects the market to keep going up doesn't mean that one has confidence in one's own understanding of the market. Even Mike Vacco doesn't think that he knows what the market will do tomorrow. We all feel confident in flipping a switch to turn on the lights, but few of us feel we

understand how the whole process works. Admittedly, some market professionals and laypersons alike claim to understand the market; but most, if pushed,
admit that they don't—even if they are willing to put their money in the market. This lack of understanding isn't a result of a shortage of "explanations" but
of their abundance. Professionals are confused by the same variety of interpretations of what makes the market tick as are lay investors. The only difference
between lay investors and professionals is that, whereas the lay investor is likely
to blame his confusion on his own inadequacy, professionals focus on the contradictions of the market itself.

Why is the market so contradictory?

These contradictions are rooted in the conflicting perspectives different persons have of the market and the different interpretations of market events that
these varying perspectives generate.

But why should the market appear so differently to different people, given
that the market seems so simple and straightforward? Stocks go up when there
are more buyers than sellers; people buy stocks, which have good earnings and
yields; companies make more money when the economy is strong. It is all
relatively simple. Furthermore, nearly all of this occurs in the public domain:
The market is a public auction. There are, moreover, fairly rigid laws to insure
that all information bearing on the market and particular stocks is made public
as promptly as possible. In short, the market would appear in many ways to be
one of the last places one would expect to find conflicting perspectives.

The key to an understanding of this apparent paradox is to recognize that
people are seldom, if ever, interested in simply knowing "what" is going on.
People want to know what is going on in order to know what is going to happen
so that they can adjust their own actions to serve their own interests—whatever
these interests might be. Knowledge serves as a guide to action.[11]

For knowledge to serve as a guide to action, however, it must tell us more
than what is going on; it must also tell us something about why and how it is
happening. This, in turn, requires a more general, theoretical grasp of the situation; the apparently simple account of what is happening must take into account and reflect the underlying structure. Different assumptions regarding
this underlying structure generate very different accounts of "what" is happening. How does one know, for example, whether there are more buyers or more
sellers? The tape doesn't record "buy" and "sell" orders; it merely records
transactions. There are hints: Did the transaction occur on an "uptick" or a
"downtick"? In the end, a judgment is still required.

Similarly, how is one to know whether the earnings and/or yields of companies are good? Are the earnings, for example, likely to continue? Has the company juggled its books?[12] Again judgment is required. Determining how a stock is "acting" or the effect of the economy on a specific company is also a question of interpretation.

Here it may be asked whether it is not true that all situations are subject to this process. The answer is obviously yes; all "reality" is an interpreted reality. What makes the market an extreme case of this general phenomenon is the peculiar feedback character that such interpretations have in the market. As a result, the market has a "self-fulfilling prophesy" character that is greater than that of most other situations. To give a concrete example:

Let us assume that we are asked to judge the relative value of two automobiles: A and B. Let us similarly assume that, for various reasons, we have a bias for A. We judge A better. We can now also assume that if we were to drive both cars, we would tend to play up the good points of A and play down its bad points. In contrast, we would be likely to do just the opposite with car B. In short, there is likely to be a self-fulfilling prophesy aspect to the way we experience the two automobiles. This aspect, however, will not change the mileage we get (though it might shade it a little), prevent a major breakdown, or stop the car from rusting. In the case of stocks, however, such predilections can affect actual performance, not just our perceptions of performance. If enough people think that a stock should be valued higher, they can push the price of the stock up by active buying, thereby fulfilling their original definition. In fact, I know of no place where the "definition of the situation" so directly and dramatically affects the situation being defined as does the stock market. It is just this quality that makes the market such an excellent area for analyzing the impact of different orientations.

Obviously the market doesn't conform to everyone's definition. If the market did what everyone thought it was going to do, we would all be millionaires many times over. The market responds to consensual definitions; it tends to conform to expectations that are held by numerous individuals.[13]

In light of the numbers of people employed in the market—more than 120,000 registered representatives and approximately an equal number of other market professionals—and the more than fifty million individual share owners, coupled with these persons' different interests and objectives, it may seem ludicrous to assert that such a consensus is possible.[14] Actually, however, such consensus is not only possible but also quite normal. The reason is that "defining the situation" and/or the "construction of social reality" is a social process, not an individual process. There are both concrete and theoretical grounds for this. To begin with the more theoretical: Whatever other benefits may be derived from imposing a meaningful order on the world, the first and foremost benefit is that it provides a basis for social solidarity. Put a slightly different way, the prime value of any meaningful view of anything is that it can be shared and hence can serve to unite people.[15] At the more concrete level, meanings are the product of social interaction; a person does not create a meaning on her own. Moreover, these patterns of social interaction are usually highly structured, with a group of experts of some sort playing central roles in maintaining the group consensus.[16] These experts are the market professionals, such as stockbrokers, stock analysts, money managers, and financial reporters. This is not to imply that lay investors have no impact on what the market does or how it is interpreted; it is only that any impact is generally filtered through the perspectives of the professionals. Even when a nonprofessional has an insight, the insight is molded to conform to a professional orientation of some sort.

What then are these professional orientations? Twenty years ago I argued that there were four basic views:

1. the Fundamentalist/Economic view;
2. the Insider/Influence view;
3. the Cyclist-Chartist view;
4. the Trader/Market Action view.

Today, for reasons that will become more apparent as we proceed, I would add two additional views:

5. The Efficient Market, with one of its variants the Enhanced Efficient Market, view; and
6. the Transformational Idea view.

Each entails what can be called its own basic "vision" of the market.

The Fundamentalist/Economic view stresses the underlying economic conditions affecting individual companies, industries, and the general economy of both the United States and the world in general.

The Insider/Influence view, in contrast, focuses upon the supply and demand factors influencing stock prices, with special interest given to those individuals and institutions that exert a disproportionate influence on the market in general.

The Cyclist-Chartist view perceives the market primarily in terms of its own patterns of behavior. It concentrates on past patterns, seeking to discover the patterns of the future.

The Trader/Market Action view notes the market movements of individual stocks and of the market as a whole. It is concerned with how specific stocks respond to specific information and overall market trends.

The Efficient Market view is actually not a new view. Twenty years ago, I discussed it in detail, describing believers in the Efficient Market theory. At that time, however, I did not include it as one of the basic market orientations, since most proponents of the view were seen as "outsiders." In brief, the view holds that the market is sufficiently efficient that the price of a given issue at any time is the most accurate assessment of the value of that issue at that time. As such, it makes little sense to those who accept the Efficient Market view to gather the types of information pursued by Fundamentalists, Insiders, Cyclists-Chartists, or Traders in an attempt to outguess the market. By and large, it also makes little sense to believers in what I have called the Enhanced Efficient Market view. In contrast to strick Efficient Market advocates, however, they believe that there are numerous small inefficiencies in the way the market assimilates and reflects information that make it possible to slightly outperform the major indexes over time. Since they also believe that it is really not possible to significantly outperform the market—remember they believe in the Efficient Market theory—they are more than willing to accept incremental increases.

The Transformational Idea view, though it shares aspects of both the Trader and Cyclist-Chartist views, does represent for me a new outlook. The essence of this perspective is that the market, or more accurately the best performing stocks, is governed by Transformational Ideas. Adherents of this view not only believe that prices reflect the general consensus of the value attributable to a given stock, but also that Transformational Ideas have the power to dramatically change such evaluations. Whereas Fundamentalists seek to *get ahead* of economic information, Insiders to *get ahead* of supply and demand information (that is, who is buying and who is selling), Cyclists to *get ahead* of pattern formations, Traders to *get ahead* of market action and momentum, and Enhanced Efficient Market believers to *minimally get ahead* of market efficiencies, supporters of the Transformational Idea view seek to get ahead of new ideas, often embodied in new technologies.

Why these six? Why not more? Why not fewer? Why not others?

For one reason, because that is the way things are, or at least appear to be for the moment. A better, more theoretical explanation is that these overviews reflect in their own way the basic intentional modes that govern human action in general. The Fundamentalist/Economic view reflects what could be called the external/physical world–pragmatic perspective; the Insider/Influence view the social-political relationship perspective; the Cyclist-Chartist and the Transformational Idea views; the symbolic meaning–ordering perspective; and the Trader/Market Action view; the experience-emotive-intuitive perspective. The Cyclist-Chartist view differs from the Transformational Idea view insofar as the former treats governing ideas as somehow independent—one might even say transcendent—forces, whereas supporters of the Transformational Idea view clearly see such governing meanings as imbedded in human consciousness. The Efficient Market believers, meanwhile, are the great eclectics, seeing all of the above factors at work. Unfortunately, they also tend to believe that one can detect these factors at work only *after* they have had their effect, not before.

When I initially introduced the first four views, I noted that it is the peculiar self-fulfilling prophecy character of the stock market that allows each of these modes full development and existence in the market, in contrast to most other social situations, which favor one or another mode over the others. Here I might add that it has been a further intensification of this self-fulfilling prophecy character of the market that has given rise to the two new types introduced above. (I shall return to this issue later.)

How these general overviews are embodied in the specific views and behaviors of individual market professionals is a more complex issue. To begin with, few individuals are completely consistent to any single overview. This is related to another, more important point, namely, that professionals use these overviews for different purposes. Nearly all market professionals, for example, have some interest in understanding the market, but those who are primarily interested in understanding the market in order to master it constitute a distinct minority; I call these goal-oriented intellectuals the "True Believers."[17] Most market professionals, in contrast, are primarily concerned with selling stocks; there are also others who are primarily interested in "explaining" the market and others who just like being "part of" the market. Even here, one must be careful not to be too strict, since most market professionals—who generally are more one type or another—have elements of each type.

In attempting to come to terms with these various overviews, however, it is best to start with those True Believers. The reason for this is that the salespeople, explainers, and players are all constrained by the views of the True Believers, since it is the True Believers who define the market while being engaged in the market. The salesperson is interested in the meaning of the market only as it helps project an image of understanding that is needed to sell stocks. The explainer is interested in the meaning of the market only as it constitutes the material to work with in order to produce an acceptable account, whereas the player is interested in the meaning of the market primarily to indicate where he or she is and was. Put slightly differently, the views of most market professionals are only fuzzy reflections of the articulated views of the True Believers. Only after we get to know these True Believers will we be able to understand the ways others use these overviews.

Determining whether a particular market professional is or is not a True Believer, unfortunately, is often difficult for the reason just given—namely, that many non-true believers sound like True Believers. They use the rhetoric of the True Believer in selling stocks and/or in attempting to "explain" why things happened the way they did. This is not a point that need concern you here; hopefully, by the time you have completed this study, you will be able to distinguish the genuine article from the imitations. For now I will take the liberty of introducing a spokesperson[18] for each of the general overviews noted above. Once we have heard a little from each, we will attempt to get to know them better.

The scene: a corner table in a Wall Street restaurant.
The time: approximately 1 P.M.
The actors: John, Hank, Bill, Sarah, David, and Ann.

John: You know, I really like the action of ABC; the market is down two points this morning and it is up a half on some pretty good volume.

Hank: Yup. I heard that Fidelity was taking a pretty big position; I also hear that one or two banks that were unloading it have completed their sales.

Bill: I think that both of you guys are crazy. How can you buy a company that is still trading at thirty-five times earnings in a market like this?

Ann: I don't know Bill, maybe John and Hank have a point. It hasn't really broken its support level throughout this decline. My charts indicate that if we get any sort of market it would be good for ten or twenty points before it runs into any sort of real selling pressure. Personally, I'd rather try DEF. Its chart looks even better.

John: Ann, I don't care what your charts say. DEF is down another two today, and it hasn't lifted at all when the market has.

Hank: I don't know, John, maybe Ann is right. I heard that two different houses will be putting out a strong buy recommendation on the whole biomedical industry and at least one of them will highlight DEF. I must admit, however, that the word is that some insiders have been lightening up on their holdings.

Sarah: Traditional biomedical companies are old hat already. If you are looking for a real play in the pharmaceuticals, you have to look at companies
that are into DNA and cloning.

Bill: I don't know from DNA, cloning, or what you call "old hat" biomedical
research, Sarah, but I can't see how DEF is any better or worse than
ABC. They are both trading at such high multiples, and it will be years,
if ever, before either will pay a dividend. How can you mess around with
them when there are hundreds of solid companies paying real dividends
and trading at under twenty times earnings—to say nothing about the
yields you can get on some bonds?

John: You might be right about the bonds, Bill, but most of those stocks you
are so hot on are real dogs. One or two of those secondary stocks you
follow have been behaving better, but most of them have shown me nothing for months. Admittedly one of those small oil companies you follow
has me a little interested. It has lifted nicely on each of the last few
rallies.

Dave: John, I really don't know what you expect them to show you that they
haven't already shown you. Just because a stock lifts today doesn't mean
it will lift tomorrow. And if I were you, Bill, I wouldn't worry so much
about high multiples. If a stock is trading at a high multiple, the market
is telling you it is worth it for one reason or another. You guys are all
always trying to outguess the market. Give it up. Go with the flow.

Hank: If you knew what I've been hearing, Dave, you'd be a little more
concerned about where the flow could take you, especially when it comes
to the small oils. I don't know what they have been showing John, but
from what I hear you'd be smart not to mess around with any of the small
oil companies right now. There are supposedly two or three pension
funds that are drowning in oil. They plan to be liquidating them for the
next six months. The word is that there are big blocks overhanging a
number of companies right now.

Ann: Hank may be right. The charts on all the oils indicate that they've got
nowhere to go but down. Even the one or two that have lifted haven't
been able to break out. If you want to go with low P/E stocks with a good
yield, I've got a few utilities that look really good to me. They could all
be good for 20 percent moves. Not only do their charts look good, but all
of them usually do very well at this time of the year.

Sarah: Ann, how can you be serious about utilities in this market? You need
to have your money in growth opportunities. Sure, utility prices may firm

and you may be able to make a few bucks, but the big money is always made in the cutting-edge companies, and there is nothing cutting edge about utilities.

John: Sarah, while I'm sympathetic to your commitment to cutting-edge companies, I have to see something in the stock action before I'm willing to make a commitment. In the case of some of the utilities, I have to agree with Ann that their recent action has been encouraging. I can't see, however, how anyone can touch any of them; they never trade in any volume. It will cost you two or three points to take even a modest position in any of them, and God help you if you ever want to get out fast.

Dave: Why are you always so worried about getting out fast? I don't see how you can ever expect to come out ahead with all of this in and out stuff. If you stick with the market, you'll come out ahead in the long run. What you need to do is just make sure that the stocks you own and your buy and sell executions give you every edge you can get.

Hank: Dave, you live in an academic, make-believe world. It makes a big difference in who is buying and who is selling. For example, while I'd go along with John and avoid most of the small oils, I've heard that XYZ is starting to get some institutional sponsorship. Two or three of the big boys have been nibbling at it for the last two months. However, the funds won't touch most of them.

Bill: If any fund touches XYZ, they're crazy. After Ann mentioned it last week, I got hold of its annual statement and its 10-K form. If you checked out footnote 6, you'd see that they're going to have to raise at least $30 million in the next few months to cover some notes coming due. I hate to think what interest rate they'll have to pay even in this market. And God forbid what could happen if the fed ever decided to increase interest rates.

Hank: You're scared of your own shadow, Bill. Believe me, if those guys are putting their money in, they must know that XYZ is going to get the necessary loan. One of those institutions had two of its top analysts down at the home offices of XYZ last month for three days going over the company from top to bottom. There must be something good going on down there if they decided to make a commitment.

John: Sure. They figure that if they buy 100,000 shares of that dog, they can drive it up five or ten points. On their quarterly statement, it will make them look awful smart. Just let them try to get out.

Dave: There you go again, worrying about getting out.

Bill: Look, John, as far as XYZ is concerned, I agree with you. It is a crummy
company, but I have to agree with Dave that you shouldn't always be so
worried about getting out. If you buy good companies with solid earnings
and a good dividend, you can always afford to hold them. By buying such
companies and holding them, you'll end up doing better than with all this
in and out stuff of yours.

Ann: I should be honest with you guys. XYZ is my stock and I think both
John and Bill are wrong, but if it rallies through 22, I'll probably sell it
since it hasn't been able to hold above the low twenties for years.

John: Well, I'll tell you, Ann, if it came through 22 in volume, I'd be tempted
to buy it despite what Bill says. Till then, I'd rather stick with those companies that are showing me something right now. Hey, it's quarter to two.
I better get back and see what's happening. I have a feeling that the
volume should pick up this afternoon.

Hank: I've got to run, too. I've got a meeting with a guy over at one of those
new hedge funds. I'm interested in finding out what they're up to.

Sarah: Hank, I can't figure you out. You're a bright guy. Why are you always
trying to find out what other people are thinking? It is easier to figure
out what people are going to think by discovering what are going to be
the exciting ideas of tomorrow.

This stylized discussion reflects the six general overviews noted earlier. Bill
favors the Fundamentalist view; Hank, the Insider view; Ann, the Cyclist-
Chartist view; John, the Trader view; Sarah, the Transformational Idea view;
and Dave, the Efficient Market view. But are these people real? Yes and no.
They are what sociologists call "ideal types"; that is, each is a prototype based
on a number of similar individuals. During the last thirty-five years, I have met
a number of Bills, Anns, Hanks, and Johns. About twenty years ago, I began to
run into a few Daves. In recent years, the Daves have flourished as fewer and
fewer professionals have succeeded in outperforming the market indexes.
Sarah is somewhat different. Nearly everyone on Wall Street has some Sarah
in them. Everyone is looking for the big idea that will make them rich. It
has namely been in recent years, however—and perhaps as a precursor in the
sixties—that serious students of the market have been willing to go with such
ideas by themselves. To a large extent this has been due to the unprecedented
rise in the market, coupled with the meteoric rise of comparatively new companies such as Microsoft, Amazon, Cisco, and biomedical companies. There is
also a sense, however, that ideas themselves seem to play a bigger role than

they did previously. Whatever the reason, one can find a good number of Sarahs on Wall Street today.

To protect the anonymity of all those who spoke to me[19] and to convey a more accurate feel for the market, I have elected to present my thoughts through these "flesh and blood" (albeit fictional) characters rather than by using a set of statistical findings. For each type, I have focused upon one individual but have camouflaged any personal characteristics by using specific traits of other adherents of the same view. All direct quotes and stated opinions, however, are authentic. Given that the conversations and observations reported in this book have occurred over a period of more than thirty-five years, however, accuracy requires that some attempt be made to catch various transitions that have happened during this period. To do this, I have elected to note when various views and positions were presented and then to update these views and positions with later statements and information where appropriate.

So far, we have had only a quick glimpse of each character. It's time we got to know them and their views of the markets better. It should be remembered that the market professionals to be described—persons with clearly articulated views of the market—are relatively few in number. Once we know the True Believers better, we shall take a closer look at the other types.

PART II

THE TRUE BELIEVERS

2

A FUNDAMENTALIST

I was introduced to Mr. Chester by one of the managing partners of his firm approximately twenty years ago. I doubt whether he would have granted me an interview without such a high-level introduction. Even then, only after it became clear that I knew something about the market did he talk to me freely. In fact, he adopted an almost paternal interest in what I was doing. As I got to know Mr. Chester better—I never did get to call him Bill—I realized that his paternalistic style was not limited to his relationship to me. It was a style he used with most of his customers and even his fellow brokers.

Bill Chester had been in the market for over forty years. He started out in the back office of one of the street's major firms right out of college during the thirties and had been a registered representative since the late thirties. Even before joining his firm, with which he remained associated until his recent retirement, he followed the market and still has clear memories of the 1929 crash. For over four decades until his retirement in the mid-eighties, he was a well established, highly respected broker. From the moment anyone meets him, they knew that they were dealing with a successful businessman. His suits are conservative but expensive, his hands are well manicured, and his manner is one of confidence. He talks quietly, but it's clear that he is not in any way meek.[20]

Mr. Chester is and always was a Fundamentalist. Others saw him as a Fundamentalist, and so did he. To Bill Chester, market values reflected economic values. This general orientation determined how he saw the market and individual companies, what he read, whom he talked to, and which stocks he bought. It also determined how he perceived the role of a registered representative.

To Bill Chester, the best indicator of the market as a whole was the Dow Jones Index. The "Dow" tells you where the real market is. It didn't bother him that the averages were heavily weighted in favor of established, "blue chip" companies; it is specifically because they are so weighted that he liked them. He wanted little or nothing to do with small, untested companies—he didn't, for that matter, want much to do with large, tested companies that trade at high multiples. He was interested only in those companies whose market values were supported by "assets." His bible was Graham and Dodd's *Security Analysis.* The stock market professional he most admired then was Warren Buffett, though my guess is that he would be more than a little concerned with the high multiples that some of Buffett's favored stocks have recently attained.

Although Bill Chester was primarily interested in the fundamentals of the companies in which he invested, he also closely observed the economy of the country as a whole. He paid a good deal of attention to general economic indicators and to government policy, which concerns were reflected in his reading habits. He read both the *New York Times* and the *Wall Street Journal* daily, although, if he could read one paper only, it would be the *New York Times.* In this he differed from the majority of Fundamentalists, but his preference was consistent with his concern for general economic news, which he saw as more important in the long run than strictly financial news.[21]

Each week, in addition to his daily papers, he read *Time, Newsweek, Barron's* and *U.S. News and Reports;* he also subscribed to *Fortune* and *Forbes.* Each weekend he sent away for numerous financial reports on individual companies. However, he had little use for any "market service." He didn't keep or follow any charts, nor did he concern himself with most technical indicators, though he did check the "Confidence Index," which compares best grade and intermediate grade bond yields, in *Barron's.* If he had been restricted to one weekly publication, he would have unhesitatingly pick *Barron's.*

His attitude toward *Barron's* reflected his attitude toward the market as a whole. He began by reading the editorials and columnists who tended to share his market orientation; after this he checked out any information and reports on individual companies carried that week. The rest of the publication he skimmed.

Although Bill Chester absorbed a tremendous amount of information, he seldom acted on it immediately. This was consistent with his view of his own role. He saw himself primarily as a financial advisor whose job it was to digest and interpret information. The information had to be of a specific type— namely, fundamental economic and political information. He believed that he first had to develop a feel for the economy and the market as a whole. If he had a positive feel, his next job was to pick those solid companies that he thought were likely to perform as well, if not better, than the market as a whole.

Bill Chester knew that his approach differed from that of most other brokers, especially younger ones. This didn't bother him, though on a number of occasions during his long career he had been upset when his more speculative colleagues made money and he didn't. As far as he was concerned, however, his more speculative colleagues were playing Russian roulette. To make things worse, they were doing it with other people's financial lives. He was fond of talking about "yesterday's hotshots" who were wiped out when the market turned against them.

This is not to imply that Bill Chester is or was a loner; he's not. He maintained close contacts with other brokers and watched carefully what his own firm and other firms were recommending. He also actively solicited the opinions of his more well-connected customers. He was only concerned, however, with certain types of information, and even then he insisted on analyzing it for himself. It was in his relationship with his customers that this aspect of Bill Chester's style was most prominent.

Bill Chester had a fairly high regard for most of his customers' market intelligence; he thought most customers are smarter than most brokers are willing to admit, though he acknowledged that his customers were probably more sophisticated than the average investor. Most of his customers, especially the most active ones, were successful businessmen, though it was not their business success per se that Bill Chester found important. Nor did he give much weight to their abilities to interpret the "tape" or their familiarity with market jargon. He based his judgments on their understanding of fundamental economic factors and their access to "good" information. He was interested in knowing what the earnings picture looked like to someone in close contact with a company. This did not mean he took such information at face value, but it was the type of information he felt that he could use.

Bill Chester's customers gave him more than information. They provided him with his living. Like most brokers, he worked on a commission basis, which can create strains for a Fundamentalist, since this approach generates less turnover of stocks than do others. The Fundamentalist generally buys stocks for the long haul. A successful Fundamentalist, consequently, requires customers with substantial sums of money to invest; furthermore, it is preferable that they regularly have new money to invest. Without such large sums, the Bill Chesters of the market can't begin to earn the commission dollars they require for their own life styles and for the requisite "image of success"; as it is, they must also rely on their own investments. Similarly, it is primarily customers with large sums of money who can profit tax-wise from long-term investments in contrast to short-term trades. There is, in short, a symbiotic relationship between the Fundamentalist's approach and the needs and resources of customers with substantial economic resources.

Bill Chester felt that the main problem with most customers was that they were lazy; they were not willing to put into the market the time and effort required. Many had sound instincts, but few had developed their critical abilities. As a result, he found that most of his customers followed his advice quite closely. This did not mean they followed him blindly. To sustain their confidence in him he had to make his position understandable to his customers. He would have been happier if his customers were as knowledgeable about the market as they were about their own businesses.

Bill Chester also had a few trading accounts for which he acted solely as an executor of orders. As he told me, "For them I can't be of much help," though he certainly was not negative toward them. Not only can such accounts generate sizable commissions but since they make their own decisions, they also are relatively undemanding. His job was simply to give them the information for which they asked. He readily admitted that, though it was not his style, some people can make money trading. He was similarly more than willing to handle accounts of individuals who invested on their own, usually as a result of their own information. In these cases he tried to find out why the customer was investing in the particular stock. It was the type of information he found useful. Questioned about this, he informed me that many of his wealthier clients, as is common with such clients, also maintained accounts with other firms. As a result, Chester was able to gather information about the thinking of other professionals with whom he did not have direct contact.

Bill Chester did not feel that all of one's moneys should be invested in stocks. His Fundamentalist orientation led him to look favorably upon numerous other forms of investments, such as bonds, real estate, and insurance. He himself had substantially more sums invested in real estate during the late sixties than he did in stocks. Furthermore, he was negative toward stock options, lettered stocks, and short selling. The ideal investment for Bill Chester was an undervalued stock of a major American corporation.

Despite being negative toward "tips," charts, and short-term trading, Bill Chester was not above using them; but he used them primarily to guide his selling, not his buying. If he heard a "tip" on a company he owned, he was likely to be a seller if it had a substantial move. Similarly, he'd likely be a seller if a company he owned began to run up after making a new high on some chart or if it became a favorite of the traders. In such cases, his view was that the stock was being pushed up by speculative fever that could not be maintained over the long run. Once the stock reached what he felt was its full value, he was happy to sell it even if this meant seeing it go higher. Bill Chester believed in the preservation of capital. If it came to a choice between speculative gains and protection of capital, he would always favor the protection of capital.

From what has been said, it should be clear that Bill Chester took the long view toward the market. He was never in a great rush to buy or sell. This was reflected in the way he made his recommendations. Though he used the telephone constantly, as do all brokers, he relied more upon the mail than most established brokers. He sent out hundreds of written reports to his own customers. He was then likely to tell his customers to think over a recommendation and to give him a call if they were interested. Furthermore, when selling, he was likely to make use of limit orders—that is, he was likely to offer his stock at a specific price rather than at the present market price. When questioned about this practice, he told me that he only bought "undervalued" stocks and was not about to lose an opportunity for a half a point; that said, when he was selling, he wanted to get what he thought the company was worth. Since he didn't aim to get the top price (he was willing to sell when he felt a company was fairly priced), he didn't worry about losing his opportunity to sell. There is the added fact that his selling tended to be more intensive than his buying.[22] Here he admitted to being a better buyer than seller, but this seems to be a general attitude of most brokers. Whereas some brokers tend to kick themselves for selling too soon, Bill Chester seldom did. As far as he was concerned, the risks involved in obtaining those last few points were just too great.

In many ways, the Bill Chesters of the market would be the ideal brokers for widows and orphans. He is both conservative and thoughtful. Unfortunately, there are few widows and orphans who are likely to obtain this kind of service unless they have substantial financial resources; moreover, Bill Chester always felt more comfortable dealing with established businessmen, since they could afford the risks that are entailed in the market. Also, these businessmen are the ones who can provide the types of information that Fundamentalists both desire and require. It's doubtful that he would have refused any account, even if it were small, but such an account would have received less attention than Bill Chester gave to his larger ones.

There were and are only a limited number of Bill Chesters, but nearly all brokers have a little of Bill Chester in them, since it's impossible to operate in the market without having some concern for the fundamentals of the market-place. To Bill Chester and his like, the fundamentals of the market *are* the market; the rest is an enigma that is best ignored.[23] As he would often say, "I don't try to mastermind the market. I am content to look for sound values and to stick with them till the market recognizes them."

This attitude tends to reinforce a general conservative outlook. There is, however, nothing passive about this approach. Bill Chester and most other Fundamentalists believe in hard work. During the later years of his career, most of this hard work entailed going over company reports, talking to people, and keeping up-to-date on all sorts of financial information. It also meant usu-ally being at his desk before eight in the morning and staying till five in the afternoon. Furthermore, though he refused to talk business during the week-end, he put in a good number of hours of reading. When he was younger, he also spent a fair amount of time on the road visiting companies, speaking to administrative and financial officers, checking out plants—gathering informa-tion.

This explains why Bill Chester tended in his later years to be less interested in small companies that often attract the interest of a number of other Funda-mentalists. It is probably fair to say, in fact, that most Fundamentalists are interested in such small companies. The reason is not hard to understand; small, unknown companies are more likely to be undervalued in a purely eco-nomic sense. Bill Chester knew this, but like any true Fundamentalist he also believed that all such companies had to be checked out in person—which he was no longer willing to do.

Bill Chester differed from most other true Fundamentalists, or at least mar-ket Fundamentalists, in other ways. To begin with, he was more interested in general economic and political events than market Fundamentalists, who give greater attention to the economic conditions affecting specific companies and industries. He also differed in how he made his living. Bill Chester was a retail broker, whereas most true Fundamentalists tend to be market analysts, finan-cial advisers, or institutional brokers. This is for the simple reason that it's difficult for a retail broker to make a living as a true Fundamentalist—you can't generate enough business. Bill Chester could afford to put his customers into bonds and long-term situations because he had substantial assets of his own; most retail brokers don't and consequently can't.

Bill Chester also differed from most true Fundamentalists, and brokers in general, in the respect he gave to his customers' opinions. After all, he had managed over a period of years to acquire a comparatively successful and so-phisticated clientele. But most market customers, he believed, are lazy, unin-formed, and simply ignorant of how the market works.

There's one other aspect of Bill Chester's view of himself that deserves some comment. He took seriously his role as financial adviser. In this respect, he was more like the old-time family banker—most of whom were also Fundamental-ists. In contrast, most of today's Fundamentalists have been sufficiently burnt by what they consider to be the greed and ignorance of their clients that they have lost their sense of responsibility. They are content to present their infor-mation and to make their recommendations, and if people want to ignore what they have to say, that's their business. Bill Chester felt, on the contrary, that it was his job to convince his customers that he was right. This was why he at-tempted to educate his customers as best as he could.

There is another important aspect of Bill Chester's attitude toward the mar-ket that should be noted. Despite his many years in the market and his success in it and his love for it, Bill Chester was never wedded to the market. When asked whether he had ever thought of getting out, he would answer, "All the time."

Nearly all true Fundamentalists, when asked that question, give a similar answer. To the true Fundamentalist, the market is only one element within a broader, more encompassing, economic system. Most true Fundamentalists I have interviewed indicated a secret longing to run a business of their own. Many are put off by what they see to be the speculative nature of the market; some are actually morally offended that people are able to make money invest-ing in stocks that are intrinsically overvalued. Most are quite happy when such persons get battered, and if the person had previously made a lot of money, they are often ecstatic. The world of business, and in some cases the academic world, exert a strong pull on many true Fundamentalists; they are seen as places where the Fundamentalist credo is held in higher respect and where its true believers are more esteemed.

Most true Fundamentalists remain critical of what they consider to be excessive market speculation, yet even the most conservative have been influenced by the dramatic rise of the market in recent years. Ironically, although most have been caught up in the overall market surge, this very surge has also served to distance them more from the market. Perhaps the best way to explain this apparently contradictory development is to see it as a reversal between fore-ground and background.

Until fairly recently, it was taken for granted that the stock market was merely one element within the total economic picture. There were also real estate, bonds, precious metals, other commodities, and of course cash. Most brokers, even fundamentally oriented brokers, consequently worked on the assumption that they were being asked to manage only a part of their customers' total assets. For decades leading up to the nineties, moreover, even highly conservative brokers commonly believed that their customers tended to be underinvested in equities. As a consequence of these assumptions, most brokers, even Fundamentalists, saw their primary responsibility as investing the money entrusted to them in sound equities.

The emergence of the stock market in recent years as the premier investment vehicle has changed things considerably. A good number of Fundamentalist brokers now see allocation of resources entrusted to them as one of their, if not the only, primary responsibilities, rather then stock selection. This trend has been reinforced by a broader move toward investing in index funds, which further serves to lessen the importance of stock selection. Even ten years ago, this might have required turning resources back to one's customers for investment elsewhere, but today most brokerage firms have sufficiently broadened the products that they now offer that this is not the case. Whereas twenty years ago there were only a few hundred mutual funds, today there are approximately as many mutual funds as there are stocks. This means that a broker can invest a client's money in numerous different ways, according to all sorts of different objectives (such as degree of risk, how much growth, types of stocks, return on capital), without having to engage in any stock selection. All the broker needs to do is select the right fund or set of funds. Moreover, most brokerage firms now offer a range of their own proprietary funds. There also exist various types of bond funds and real estate issues. This exponential growth in investment products has served to transform the possibilities open to today's Fundamentalists. Though many, if not most, still seek to discover undervalued equities in which to invest their own and their clients' resources, they have the added opportunity to earn a living and to be true to their own beliefs by allocating their clients' resources among a wide range of investment forms. The recent growth in what are called wrapped accounts, in which a broker, now a financial manager, receives a set percentage—usually 1 percent of an annual 2 percent fee—for managing an account, has also made this approach financially rewarding for the broker/financial manager.

In light of the above, it might appear the Fundamentalist has weathered the recent changes in the market quite well. To the extent that new products and new remuneration policies have emerged, this is true. Nevertheless, there are certain clouds on the horizon that should be noted. Among the other developments in the market in recent years, there has also been a tremendous growth in technology that has dramatically enhanced the accessibility of knowledge. The Fundamentalist, like all True Believers, is highly dependent upon his or her access to relevant information and analyses. In fact, as we will see, information is the lifeblood of all True Believers and consequently the market itself. Where the various types of True Believers differ from each other is in the types of knowledge they most covet and rely upon. In many ways, the Fundamentalist is the one who has been most affected by the technological changes noted above. Today, the company and analyst reports a Fundamentalist's lifeblood—are on the Internet almost immediately upon release. Even the recommendations of a broker's firm are likely to reach major clients as quickly as they reach the broker. The good Fundamentalist can still normally bring some value-added insights to such reports, but many worry that this might change. With more and more sophisticated search engines and analytical programs available, customers, especially institutional customers, may begin to balk at the cost of also supporting a broker/salesperson, no matter how sophisticated and/or responsible that person might be.

There is one other worry that plagues many a Fundamentalist. Despite, or perhaps more accurately because of, the dramatic rise of the stock market in recent years and the wealth they and their customers have accumulated, the great majority of the Fundamentalists I have talked to in recent years reflect Bill Chester's concern for the future. As one very successful institutional salesman said to me recently, "Most of these people have never seen a real—a year or more—bear market. They think stocks can only go up. Too many people are putting too much money in this market. When it goes down, and it will go down, I fear it may make the 1929 sell-off seem mild. We will probably avoid the type of depression that 1929 brought on because we have the fed today and they can control interest rates, but a lot of people are going to get very hurt. There is no avoiding it. The market in the end responds to fundamentals, and the fundamentals dictate that no market can keep growing at a better than 20 percent annual rate."

Spoken like a true Fundamentalist.

3

AN INSIDER

Henry Strong had been involved with the market for approximately twenty-five years when I first met him in the late seventies. He was commissioned into the army upon graduation from college during the Second World War; he then spent a few years in Washington assigned to the Pentagon in the field of military procurements. He retired as a lieutenant colonel in 1948 and went to work for a large aircraft company. He says his work was mostly in public relations, but from some of his comments, it's quite clear that he was primarily a lobbyist. In the early fifties, he joined an institutional house as a defense industry analyst, but switched within a few months to institutional sales.

Hank—Henry Strong is Hank to just about everyone—asserts that as a young man, he had no interest in the market. He had a very successful uncle who, he recalls, was very much involved with the market. This uncle owned a successful hardware company, but he spent more time playing the stock market than running his business. Hank remembers his uncle always talking to him about the market, but claims that he never paid much attention to what his uncle had to say. He didn't develop any real interest in the market until he started to work for the aircraft company: some stock options came with the job. Soon, he found himself spending time trying to figure out why his options went up one day and down the next. This led to his more general interest in the market and his decision to become a market professional.

The market did well by Hank. He never acquired the personal assets of Bill Chester, but he made a very good living. This was reflected in his well dressed, well groomed, if somewhat flashy appearance. It was also highlighted by the expensive cigars that at that time he was always offering.

Hank described himself as a conduit of information. In a very real sense, that was what he was and what nearly all Insiders are. As an institutional sales-man, his job was to bring the analysts of his firm into contact with the analysts of the funds, banks, and trusts with whom he dealt. Hank's self-image, how-ever, differed from that of institutional salesmen, who see themselves as backup personnel responsible for providing tangential services.[24] Hank consid-ered what he did to be central. To Hank, the market lives on information, and information was his game.

With a number of major firms now providing voice mail from their top analysts to all of their major accounts, it is considerably more difficult for an Insider today to manage information as did Hank during his heyday. The key, however, remains keeping abreast of information as best you can. As far as Hank was concerned (and the true Insiders of today), the so-called underlying value of a company doesn't mean much. The only thing that matters is sponsor-ship. "It doesn't matter how much money a company makes; it only matters how much people are willing to pay for it." Once, over a drink, he confided, "I deal with the best analysts in town. Every week I get a dozen or so reports; some of them run over a few hundred pages. And you know what? They are wrong as often as they are right."

This doesn't mean that Hank was uninterested in what the analysts, or at least some analysts, had to say. His secret was to focus on those analysts who swung some weight. If he could bypass the analysts entirely and find out di-rectly what the "boys with the money" were going to do, so much the better. He quickly added that it doesn't always work out. "More than once, I thought I had the inside track on a stock, only to find out that there were bigger guns on the other side."

Throughout most of his market career, Hank focused upon those factors that he felt affected the supply and demand forces at work in the market. His bread and butter, however, remained the information that he was able to ac-quire through his many contacts. He followed bond yields closely because they compete with stocks, net redemption figures of various mutual funds because they indicate the amount of public money involved in the market, and the international money scene because it reflects funds flowing in and out of the United States.[25] If he didn't have so much time and energy already invested in his personal contacts, he regularly claimed that he would give these factors even more attention. "Next year, when I have more time," he used to say, "I'm going to do more work in these areas."

Hank's interest in these factors was, however, more theoretical than actual. He was quick to point out, for example, that it is difficult, if not impossible, for him or anyone else to get an edge when it comes to these things. "There may be some people who can get this type of information early, but I haven't run into any of them yet." There was the added fact that while he "knew" that these factors affect the overall supply and demand for stocks, it is very difficult to figure out how specific facts affect specific stocks. As a result, Hank was destined to rely, as he had in the past, upon his contacts. He was also more at home working with people than with written reports.

Hank's "auction" view of the market directly influenced the way he looked at a number of other things. He was very down on the small investors. It was not that he thought they were stupid; it was just that he thought the market is stacked against them. "In the market, there has to be a buyer for every seller and a seller for every buyer. The little guy almost by definition is forced to work against the big boys. The little guy might be right, but the big boys have the money. Each year with the growth of institutional players this becomes more and more the case. As a result, most small investors just can't win." He didn't have a much higher opinion of professionals, especially retail brokers. "They're just as much in the dark as lay investors."

I was especially interested in Hank's attitude toward market manipulation. Here Hank tended to hedge. "In the old days, there was a fair amount of it; moreover, if you had an inside track you could do pretty well. Today, you really can't. There are some small companies that can still be manipulated, but with all the regulations it's impossible to do it with any of the major companies, and it is the major companies with which I have to work when dealing with large institutional accounts."

This attitude was directly related to Hank's pet peeve. When asked what he disliked most about the market, he quickly answered, "government regulation." He felt that such regulations were fine insofar as they limit outright manipulations, though he had his doubts as to how successful they were. However, he felt they unfairly tied his own hands. "Anyone could do what I do if they wanted to put the time and energy into it. Here I am out there hustling, and some guy who just sits back and waits gets the information as soon as I do." But he didn't see that there was anything wrong with someone taking advantage of information acquired by hard work.

His resentment against the government was also based on what he felt was the excessive power of the Federal Reserve. He felt that by controlling interest rates and the supply of money, the fed had too much influence over the market. "I wouldn't mind so much if their decisions weren't political in nature.

They don't juggle things to make a pile for themselves, but the results are pretty much the same."

Despite all of his reservations, Hank continued to hustle. Unlike Bill Chester, Hank spent relatively little time at his desk. He averaged at least two or three appointments a day, including usually a lunch meeting or a dinner meeting. More often than not they were social rather than formal meetings. At least three or four nights a week he entertained someone, and when Hank entertained, he did it right. During an average year, he spent more on entertainment than many brokers earn. Moreover, he was not above providing female companionship.[26]

Hank's attitude toward his own firm was characteristic of most Insiders. "The House for which you work is very important, but not for the information generated by the House. If you have good contacts, you can get the reports of other Houses as fast as you can get your own. What is important is the image of the House. You want to work for a firm that has a sound reputation; your firm's reputation helps you to make contacts. When I call a new company and say that this is Henry Strong from _____, I am much more likely to get through to a top man than if I said this is Henry Strong from Joe Blows Associates.

Though most active Insiders still take pride in their ability to "reach" a wide range of people, the type of contacts that Hank prized have been offset to a large extent by the general proliferation of information. Though Hank was primarily interested in information, he also had certain decided preferences when it came to stocks. Hank Strong liked "growth" stocks—more accurately, he liked a stock with a story. It was these types of stocks in which Hank invested his own money. He felt that the ideal company was one that had a solid financial base and something "coming down the line," a company that could stimulate some interest and thereby develop institutional sponsorship. In his day-to-day operations, he kept an especially sharp ear out for this type of story. When he got one, however, he was more likely to invest for himself than pass on the information. He explained this by noting that his institutional accounts were not interested in a company unless it already had significant institutional support. He could also find himself in a very touchy situation if it was discovered that he was pushing a stock that he had just bought himself.

Despite his various reservations about he market, Hank Strong liked the market and had been quite successful. He had developed numerous contacts and knew how to use them. His very success caused him some difficulties, however. His style put him in constant jeopardy of getting involved in potentially illegal situations. As a result, he played down his own view of the market and his own behavior. Though he told me many times that inside information was his game, he would not admit this in public. I knew about his style from other sources before I ever met him. When I first asked him about his use of inside information, however, he looked at me with what could only be called a shocked expression and said that if he did that he would end up in jail. He often introduced this theme after he had told me how he did use inside information, or at least information that was not commonly known.

This fear limited Hank's ability to spread the gospel of the Insider. It has the same chilling effect on Insiders today. In contrast to Bill Chester and the Fundamentalist, who are constantly preaching the Fundamentalist's credo, Hank and other Insiders seldom preach their views. They function more like an eastern guru than a western priest. Insiders seldom seek out converts and will "teach" and "share" only those who have passed through various tests; potential disciples and associates must be known and trusted, and must present themselves. But present they do. Hank Strong, for example, was continually questioned by people who wanted to know what he knew and how he knew it. In such situations, Hank generally limited himself to trading information. As he said, "My business is information, inside information. It doesn't make any sense for me to give it away for nothing. It makes even less sense letting people know how I got it."

Hank Strong's hesitancy to preach the Insider credo was and is not unusual for successful True Believers of the Insider view. The Insider view, consequently, is not really spread by the successful. The Insider credo, or at least a variation of it, is rather promulgated by the semi- or unsuccessful. We shall meet one such character later.

Before leaving Hank Strong, however, one further point should be noted. Hank Strong was pessimistic about his own future in the market. He saw the market becoming more and more regulated, and nearly twenty years ago he was already beginning to feel cramped. This did not lead to any conversion bearing on his view of the market. He firmly believed throughout his entire career that supply and demand forces would govern the market of the future. Furthermore, as long as he was in the market—like Bill Chester, he retired only recently—he remained a True Believer. He knew that he could have refocused his energies in the direction of sales—that is, to use his information to sell stocks rather than to beat the market. Moreover, he knew that this was the way most so-called Insider types worked. For better or worse, however, Hank Strong's basic concern, as with other True Believers, was to master the market.

He mentioned once in passing that if he couldn't continue to play the game as he wanted to, he might become a financial writer of some sort.

Hank Strong has retired, but one can still find a number of Insiders in the market. Like Hank, they continue to complain about excessive regulations and are very careful what they say to strangers. This is not surprising, because their actions and views make them highly vulnerable to a wide range of actions. Some market changes have, as Hank feared, made it more and more difficult for the Insider to function. The major exchanges are today subject to a much higher degree of self-regulation and visibility. Every trade is not only instantaneously recorded but also available to review and analyze nearly as quickly.[27] There are also such things as voice mail from analysts and services such as *First Call* (that reproduce nearly all reports within a day or so that they go public) that make it more difficult for the Hank Strongs of today to maintain their edge.

At the same time, though, other changes have opened up new vistas for Insiders. As with the Fundamentalists, these changes involve the emergence of new products, albeit quite different ones. Whereas Fundamentalists look to mutual funds and a range of nonequity products—products that offer greater diversity and lower risk—Insiders favor options and futures, which, because of their leverage, entail both greater risk and greater reward.[28] Not only do these products allow for a much greater return on capital in a short period of time, such transactions are sometimes easier to hide.[29]

Although Insiders respond to market changes in different ways from Fundamentalists, they share the Fundamentalists' concerns regarding the way information is disseminated. For the Insider, like the Fundamentalist, information and its analysis are the bread and butter of life. The type of information may be different, but it is nevertheless subject to the same technological developments. Information on institutional and insider[30] buying and selling once took days to weeks to percolate through the market, yet such information can today often be found on the Web in a matter of minutes. All of this makes it that much harder for the Hank Strongs of today to survive trading in what might be considered public knowledge. Unfortunately for the Hank Strongs of today, the risks of trading in truly insider information are extremely high. So, though Insiders continue to flourish on Wall Street, like Fundamentalists they continue to wonder about their own professional futures.

4

A CYCLIST-CHARTIST

Ann Klein is a Cyclist-Chartist—others see her as a Cyclist-Chartist, and so does she.[31] She doesn't just use and keep charts; she lives for her charts. To Ann Klein, her charts are the market. This doesn't mean that she believes anyone who can get hold of her charts will be able to understand and predict the market. Her charts are hers, and only she or someone with her interpretive skills can grasp what the charts say. To her the charts reflect not only the mysteries of the market, but also entail their own inherent complexities, much like a giant unsolved jigsaw puzzle.

Ann Klein is in her mid-thirties and has been a registered representative for a comparatively short time: seven years. For almost eight years prior she was an accountant. Even now, she looks more like the stereotype of an accountant than a stockbroker. She tends to wear modestly priced suits and dresses, which tend to border on the informal. Usually she has a pencil stuck behind her ear and her glasses always seem to be falling off. She tends to run rather than walk. She always seems to be carrying sheets of papers filled with numbers and charts.

Ann has followed the market since she was thirteen and has been in love with it for nearly all of this time. Even when she was an accountant, she spent hours every week following it. Presently, the market—except for her family of origin, with whom she still lives—is nearly her whole life. (She does have a steady boyfriend, whom she expects to marry shortly.) She arrives at her desk between eight and eight-fifteen in the morning and stays until five or six in the afternoon. She spends between three and four hours more going over her charts in the evening; much of her weekend is also spent with her charts. She can talk about the market for hours and never seem bored.

This passion for the market is derived from her firm conviction that the market—or, more accurately, individual stocks—exhibit definable activity patterns; patterns that, through hard work and study, can be grasped. To grasp these patterns is not just Ann Klein's vocation but her avocation.

To Ann Klein, the market has a life of its own. She admits that the market is affected by economic factors and buying and selling pressures; she insists, however, that it's much more than this. The market, as a result of its own rhythms, has the ability to counteract and modify economic factors and buying and selling pressures. The market even has the ability to redefine economic information and to control buying and selling pressures.[32] Consequently, to understand what the market will do, it is necessary to understand the market itself. This is what Ann Klein attempts to do.

She asserts that the market is usually at least six months ahead of the economy. Where the Fundamentalist sees this as due to the market's ability to *predict* future economic developments, Ann Klein gives greater weight to the market's ability to *determine* future economic conditions. Similarly, though she realizes that the movement of the market is based on buying and selling pressures, she sees these pressures as themselves based on the movement of the market. It makes more sense to her, thus, to focus on the market patterns than on economic factors or buying and selling pressures.

She is quick to point out: "The market is not easily understood. It demands a particular form of expertise. This expertise is not acquired easily. Each stock has its own particular rhythm. Furthermore, these rhythms are themselves difficult to fathom. Stock movements can be misleading; in fact, it is characteristic of stocks to mislead. One must know what to look for and what to ignore. It is almost as if each stock had a logic and spirit of its own. As a result, only those with the ability and willingness to work can hope to be successful."

Ann Klein's view regarding the basic complexities of the market determines her general style and outlook. To Klein, nearly all customers, her own included, have no understanding of the market. Moreover, they have little chance for gaining such understanding. "Most customers simply don't have the time, interest, nor ability to become knowledgeable. The more they think they know, the less they actually know. Furthermore, it's less than useless to try to educate them. The job of the registered representative is to make them money, not to educate. The more they know, or think they know, the more trouble they are." In this regard, Ann Klein finds physicians to be the worst group to deal with. (I might just note, however, that this is a widely held opinion among market professionals.)

Ann Klein's view of her fellow registered representatives is not much different than her view of customers. "They're ignorant and don't know what they are doing. Most registered representatives are no more than order takers. They relay to their customers what they hear; they have no more idea about what the market is going to do than their customers. They swamp their customers with company reports, stories, market jargon, etc., and hope to do a little business. More often than not, they believe in what they are saying when they say it, but if the market goes against them, they will have a new story the next day. Furthermore, most registered representatives are lazy and do not do their homework." She has a similarly negative opinion of most analysts.

What then does Ann Klein look for in the market? On what does she base her charts? In the jargon of the street, she relies on "technical information." More specifically, her charts are drawn, or more accurately computed (since Ann is a computer addict), in terms of the actual movement of stocks, the volume at which they trade, ratios of volume on advances versus volume of declines, support levels, ratio of upticks to downticks, and on and on. She keeps data on the relationships between individual companies and various market indices, and is also interested in put-call ratios, short ratios, and other ratios. How she actually combines all this information is Ann Klein's secret.

Ann Klein's view of herself as a market expert, coupled with her present position—a moderately successful broker in a fairly large office—generates certain tensions. Whereas most Bill Chesters and Hank Strongs are basically content with what they are doing, Ann Klein would like to change her role. At the present time she mainly services small accounts, but she feels this greatly limits her. Not only does it limit the amount of money she can make, it also restricts her visibility as a true market expert. She would very much like to be in a position to handle large sums of money where she could prove her own theories. She wouldn't do things differently, but she would get the recognition that she feels she deserves.

Where Fundamentalists act in response to economic factors and Insiders act in response to "stories" and "inside information," Ann Klein acts in response to the market itself. This forces her to be a seller more than do the styles of Bill Chester and Hank Strong. When Fundamentalists and Insiders buy, they are willing to wait; in fact, they expect to wait: in one case, the Fundamentalist, the purchase is based on the assumption that a value is being overlooked; in the case of the Insider, the information is private. Bill Chesters and Hank Strongs realize that they may make mistakes, but it is only over a period of time that such mistakes become obvious. Even then, they are never sure that tomorrow they won't be proven right. Ann Klein's situation is very different; if she isn't proven right, she's proven wrong, because she buys only when the market tells her that a stock is going to go up. If it doesn't go up, it means she read her charts incorrectly. In addition, Ann Klein's more technical approach tends to give her clearer sell signals than do the approaches of Bill Chester and Hank Strong. (Insiders like Hank Strong sometimes get a clear sell signal— word that there is a major sell order about to be executed. Such sell signals, however, are not nearly as common as are the technical sell signals for Ann Klein.)

Because the Cyclist-Chartist approach favors neither buying nor selling. Ann Klein is more a trader than were Bill Chester or even Hank Strong. Bill Chester and Hank Strong would sell, but only in response to information with long-term implications. Bill Chester was looking for long-term economic trends; Hank Strong followed big money, which likewise is long-term oriented. Ann Klein follows the market itself, which, by its nature, exhibits short-term fluctuations. It is not that Ann Klein's charts don't tell her about long-term trends, it's just that they are better at telling her about short-term ones. More-over, it's difficult for her to ignore those short-term signals regardless of what she sees as the long-term trend, especially when theoretically she should be able to buy back in when the stock is ready to resume its upward move.

Ann Klein justifies her trading primarily in terms of her concept of market risk. Whereas Fundamentalists and Insiders see market risk in terms of the amount of money their customers can afford to lose, Ann Klein sees risk inherent in every investment. There will always be opportunities to make money, as far as Klein is concerned; the problem is to minimize trading losses. She admits that her approach tends to generate more commissions than other approaches, but claims that this is not why she trades. If her charts favored a long-term approach, she would invest long term. It is Ann Klein's view that the problem with most Cyclist-Chartists is that they try to go long term when their charts just don't provide them with the type of information to make this possible.

One of the most interesting characteristics of Ann Klein and other Cyclist-Chartists is their attitude toward their own fallibility. On the one hand, they tend to be highly arrogant; they know what is going on and others do not. On the other hand, when they make a mistake, they are much more apt to accept the responsibility for the mistake. Bill Chester and other Fundamentalists tend to blame their mistakes on the stupidity or greed of others; "They just don't know a good buy when they see it," or "They are driving that stock out of sight and it isn't worth anything." Hank Strong and other Insiders are more likely to see it in terms of "the breaks of the game." Ann Klein, in contrast, is likely to say, "I made a mistake. I should have given more weight to the advance/decline ratios," or "I went too soon; it really hadn't tested the bottom," or "Those two tests were in hindsight really a single test." This is not surprising: if she isn't wrong (if the mistake was not hers), then the charts must be wrong, and if they are wrong, then she has nothing.[33]

This need to perfect her charts forces Ann Klein to work and rework her charts to make them conform to what happens. Each wrong prediction requires going back and discovering where she made the wrong interpretation. Ann Klein doesn't resent the demands put upon her by her approach. She knows that few other brokers work as hard as she does, but in her own words, "I find working on my charts to be more fun than TV."

Ann Klein's "arrogance" is offset not only by her willingness to accept responsibility for her own mistakes but also by a general wariness of the market itself. Though she is critical of most customers and registered representatives, she does not ignore the trends that these people generate. Bill Chester tried to ignore the general psychological tide of the market, but Ann Klein tries to go with the tide, as did Hank Strong. Ann Klein responds to public reports, in fact, much like an Insider. Though Fundamentalists tend to be "above" most such reports, Ann Klein, like an Insider, is interested in judging their impact. If they seem to be having an impact, you go with them. Whereas Insiders are likely to prejudge the impact of a report based on who put it out, Ann Klein will wait till she sees the report's impact on the market itself. In both cases, however, there is a willingness to go along. As Ann Klein continually says, "You can't fight a trend. Price movements tell you not only what the market has done and is doing, but what it will do." She doesn't care if people are buying and selling the "wrong" stocks, only that they are buying and selling. In this respect, her attitude is just the reverse of most Fundamentalists and Insiders. She doesn't care about anything until it has had an effect. Another way of saying this is that nothing—we are talking here primarily about types of information—exists until it is reflected in the market.[34]

Ann Klein's approach would seem well suited for shorting stocks. When questioned about this, she indicates a degree of uneasiness. Theoretically, she agrees; as a matter of historical fact, however, she has had some difficulty in shorting, though she told me she had started to short some recently and thought that she would be doing more short selling in the future. (This state-

ment was made with the Dow trading around the 9000 mark in mid-1998.) I
questioned her about the possibilities of buying stocks making new highs and
shorting them when they made new lows, this being a Chartist/technical mode
that some non-Chartists use. Klein felt that this was not a sound Chartist principle, since new highs and new lows by definition mean that the stock is moving
into unfamiliar grounds. She personally would much rather trade stocks within
known boundaries. Again, it seemed to be a case of following past patterns of
the market rather than attempting to predict new, future patterns.

Given Ann Klein's confidence in her own ability to read the market, I was
somewhat surprised to discover that she did relatively little trading for herself.
Her answer, however, made fairly good sense, at least from her perspective.
She stressed that she had to be objective. "I can't fall in love with any particular
company. If I owned a stock, it would impair my objectivity. I would be looking
for signs that it would go up. Furthermore, if I traded my own account, I would
have more difficulties with some of my customers. They go along with me as
long as they are making money, but they balk as soon as they are forced to take
a loss. If it was known that I did a lot of trading for myself, some customers
might become suspicious."

Many customers are suspicious of their brokers. It is considered a professional hazard. Such suspicions are more dangerous to Ann Klein than they are
to many other brokers, because Ann Klein's approach often requires that she
act immediately. A stock might drop into a buy range and then move out of it
again in a matter of minutes. If she can buy the stock in the proper range, she
can limit her potential loss; on the other hand, if she has to chase the stock,
the risk becomes too great. Consequently, Ann Klein must be able to make a
phone call and get an okay in a matter of minutes. If her customers are dubious
of her recommendation for any reason, the probabilities are that there will be
no transaction.

Though Ann Klein relies primarily on the phone for soliciting buy and sell
orders, she also makes use of the mail and personal contacts, especially when
things are slow, not so much to solicit orders as to solicit accounts. She doesn't
focus on specific stocks, but upon her own expertise. She attempts to present
herself as the "expert," not as a friend who happens to be a broker. The market
itself is her love, and she makes no bones about it. She would like to have you
along as a customer; she can use the commissions. If it is a choice between
your views and her expertise, however, your views are going to come in second.

This doesn't mean that she won't execute any order that you give her; she
will. It is just that if all you want is someone to execute your orders, then you

really don't need Ann Klein. Furthermore, though Ann Klein can use your commission, she is more interested in proving her expertise, which she cannot do if you don't follow her. In fact, one gets the clear impression that Ann Klein would be happier if the market wasn't corrupted by all those people trying to make money.

This attitude, coupled with her strong desire to prove herself, often makes Ann Klein feel like a duck out of water. This feeling of being an outsider is further fueled by the fact that women are still under-represented on Wall Street. She speculates sometimes about working for some mutual or hedge fund, where she could be freer to put her ideas into practice. She also wonders if she wouldn't be happier working as a technical analyst for someone else. I have no doubt that at the first opportunity she will do one or the other.

In this regard, Ann Klein is similar to most other true believers in the Cyclist-Chartist credo. Probably less than 25 percent function as brokers, but I have presented Ann Klein as a broker because brokers were responsible for most of the statements attributed to her.

Though Ann Klein has been described as a Cyclist-Chartist, she is clearly more a Chartist than a Cyclist. There is nevertheless a strong Cyclist quality to her view of the market. Ann Klein uses her charts as technical tools but she sees them as much more; she truly believes that there are underlying patterns to the market. Her charts work only insofar as they accurately grasp these underlying patterns. Ann Klein clearly does not see herself as merely a technician; neither does she characterize her approach as a purely technical approach. Most purely technically oriented analysts see themselves as trying to impose some order on a basically disordered universe (that is, the market); in this regard, they have more in common with Traders, who will be discussed shortly, than with Cyclist-Chartists. Ann Klein sees herself as trying to discover a very real order that underlies the market.

The belief that there is an underlying, or transcendent, order to the market is more characteristic of what may be called the universal Cyclist-Chartists. Here we confront a most unique group. What distinguishes them from analysts like Ann Klein is their concern for nonmarket, and even noneconomic, factors that influence market cycles. These persons are interested not only in inherent patterns of the market, but also in such things as seasonal patterns, moon cycles, and similar phenomena, which they see affecting the market.

The reasons they present in support of their views depend upon which nonmarket cycles they use. Those who emphasize moon cycles tend to talk about underlying biological-psychological forces; those who stress historical rhythms tend to talk about general economic-political forces. In all cases, however, they see market cycles as reflecting other, more "basic" cycles.

Though such persons exist, their numbers are few. I mention them because even more than the Ann Kleins, they deeply believe in an underlying order that is the essential element in the Cyclist-Chartist world view. They also deserve mention, because they do have an impact upon the general mind of the market. Even persons who think that such views of the market are nonsense tend to incorporate some of their elements. We have, for example, such notions as "summer rallies," or the idea that January will reflect the movement of the market for the whole year. In some cases, it can be argued that there are political/economic factors at work, but more often than not such patterns are accepted as having a force of their own. In addition, I should just add that, though there are few who truly believe in such patterns, they control much more money than one might guess. I know of at least three funds that are controlled, at least in part, by such Cyclists.

This concern with some underlying or transcendent order clearly distinguishes what I have called the true Cyclist-Chartist from those who simply use charts and other technical information. For the true, believing Cyclist-Chartist, technical information is merely a tool for discovering governing patterns. For those called market technicians, such charts and technical information tend to be indicators of a wide range of activities and factors. What irks a number of true believing Cyclist-Chartists is that modern computer technology has served to generate and make available a continual supply of charts and other data that appear to be the work of Cyclist-Chartists, but that have little to nothing to do with their true views.

All True Believers, compared to the great majority of those who are not True Believers, reflect a similar passion for their particular vision of the market. This gives rise to what can only be called a deep ambivalence toward the nitty-gritty of the concrete markets. It is almost as if the daily nitty-gritty corrupts their grand vision. This explains why so many True Believers, even quite successful ones, regularly fantasize about stepping back from the market. Cyclist-Chartists probably reflect this tendency more than any other type of True Believer. Moreover, the growth of technical service companies and increased reliance on technical information have made it possible for a good number of Cyclist-Chartists to act on this predilection. In fact, though it is really impossible to prove it, I would guess that presently only a minority actually function as registered reps.

A TRADER

John Holland belongs to a rapidly diminishing breed: he is a successful Trader. To John Holland, the market is a game—a very serious game, but a game nevertheless. He often talks of the market as if it were a reflection of the game of life. As such, he sees it as incorporating all of the elements that concern Bill Chester, Hank Strong, and Ann Klein. To him, the market reflects economic values, buying and selling pressures, and rhythms and patterns of its own. In addition, he gives great weight to the role of chance. All of these things are combined to generate what he calls the "feel" of the market. To master it requires intellect, intuition, and hard work. The payoff is that the market offers rewards, both financial and psychological, which can be obtained nowhere else.

Listening to him talk about the market, you might conclude that John has had an interest in it, if not a love, since he was young. Such is not the case; to all intents and purposes, John Holland fell into the market by accident. As a young man he had no knowledge of the market; the financial pages were those pages between the sports section and the funnies. Neither he nor anyone in his family ever owned any stocks. After graduating from college with high honors, he earned a master's in history, spent some time in the armed service, worked for the government, and traveled. He was first exposed to the market during this period by a wealthy acquaintance who suggested that he buy a few shares of a company that the acquaintance thought was due for a substantial rise. John bought them and made some money. He reinvested his profits and began to follow the market. He began to read books on the market and to develop his own orientation. He found that he really enjoyed the market and that he had a good, natural feel for it. He became a broker, a very successful broker.

You would be unlikely to recognize John's success on first meeting with him; he does not project the aura of wealth and influence that one immediately senses from a Bill Chester or a Hank Strong. There is a casualness about John Holland that can be very misleading. He dresses well but not in an obviously expensive or flashy style; he speaks clearly and with some authority, but he's not overwhelming. There is an impish quality about him.

This impish quality is directly related to John's view that the whole market is one big game. It is an important game, because you play it with real money, but the game is more important than the money. This was clearly revealed to me once, when he pulled a jumble of bills from his pocket. He noticed me looking at him and laughed. "You can see from the way I carry my money, that I'm not overly concerned with money per se. To operate the way I do, you can't be."

John Holland realized almost from the beginning that if he had any special ability vis-à-vis the market, it was his feel for it. Others had better and more information, but he was better able to interpret such information and to apply it. He could do this because he was more tuned into the emotive, psychological mood of the market. He found that the information of others took on new meanings for him, meanings that seemed to allow him to make better use of the information than those from whom he received the information. He found that the market did not respond to all earning reports in the same way. Some reports were ignored; others were not. Similarly, the market responded differently to different types of stories. There were even differences in the way different stocks responded technically. In all of these cases, he found that the best guide to what the market would do was what the market was doing.

John Holland gave me some example as to what he meant by "feel for the market." "Take earnings. You always want to buy a company with good earnings, but more important than the earnings in and of themselves is the growth in earnings. Two companies may be earning a dollar, but if one company has been earning a dollar for years and it looks like that is what they will be earning for years to come, the market will price its stock differently from a company that last year earned seventy-five cents and the year before that fifty cents, but may earn a dollar fifty next year. It is not earnings themselves that matter so much as earnings plus price-earning ratios. Even then there are differences between companies. Some companies are able to catch the imagination of the street; others are not.

"The same is true for buying and selling pressures. With some stocks it really doesn't matter that a big fund is buying or selling; it doesn't change the picture. There are other stocks where an institutional buy or sell changes everything. Similarly, there is some buying that can be the kiss of death to a stock. On the other hand, information that some institution is unloading a large block may be bullish since the stock may have been depressed because everyone knew there was a large block overhanging it. You have to have a feel for what is going on.

"I feel the same way toward most technical information. The trouble with most Chartists and other technicians is that they take themselves and their indicators too seriously. Sometimes a stock will make a new high or a new low and it doesn't mean anything. A recommendation may just have come out that nudged it out of its normal trading range. Or a stock may be affected by a big order from some fund. At other times, you can almost see the buying coming in. You have to learn to go with the tape; you can't fight it. That doesn't mean you try to catch every swing; you would go bankrupt doing that. It is hard to explain, but if you pay attention, you get a feel for what's going on."

John Holland relies mainly on his intuition, but he is constantly educating his intuition. He spends nearly as much time studying the market as Ann Klein does. Where Ann Klein spends most of her time with her charts, John Holland is into everything. He reads the same reports that Bill Chester reads; like Hank Strong, he follows the activity of large institutions and keeps a constant eye on a range of technical indicators. In addition, he spends a good deal of time simply thinking about the market, the economy, and the world as a whole. He is constantly trying to get the pulse of the market; he wants to know what the market is responding to and why.

To a large extent, John Holland tries to combine the best elements of Bill Chester's, Hank Strong's, and Ann Klein's approaches. There are drawbacks to this. By its very nature, John Holland's approach is highly complex. He faces the constant danger of being overwhelmed by information. To avoid this, he seeks to simplify the information that he acquires. He must remind himself every day of what's important and what's unimportant. In doing this, he again relies upon his own feel for the market. This does not mean that he has no general rules; he has, but each rule must be interpreted in the context of the market as it is at that moment.

John Holland is, if anything, a stronger advocate of the short-loss theory than Ann Klein. Ann Klein will let her charts tell her when she must take a small loss, but John Holland will make use of a variety of indicators. He may sell a stock at a loss that is actually going up in price if he feels that its action is not good compared with the rest of the market. In contrast, he may ride a stock down through a support level if he feels that the stock's bad performance can be accounted for by the action of the market as a whole. He is also more likely to buy a stock making a new high than is Ann Klein. One of John Holland's market aphorisms is "Buy high, sell higher."[35]

John's willingness to buy high-priced stocks is in direct contrast to Bill Chester's philosophy that could be summed up by the more familiar aphorism, "Buy low, sell high."[36] John Holland is not only willing to pay high for a stock (from a historical point of view), but would actually prefer to. He wants to be with the market leaders. He argues that the market leaders—stocks trading in volume and making new highs—almost always outperform the market as a whole. As a result, he has historically favored *glamour stocks* with high multiples. It isn't that he is uninterested in earnings, only that he feels that the market has decreed that stocks with earning growth are entitled to a higher multiple than stocks with limited growth. "Ideally," he says, "what you want to find is a stock that is experiencing such growth in earnings for the first time. If you can find such a stock, you will not only get the move based on the growth in earnings but a play on the change in multiple assigned to the stock." This does not mean that he is wedded to glamour stocks. If market leadership is taken over by cyclical companies, John Holland will be buying cyclicals.

In many ways, John Holland is a skeptic. He seeks out company statements, but he never accepts the conclusions of a statement without reading all the footnotes. He is interested in knowing who is recommending what and who is buying what, but he seldom acts in response to such recommendations. He is more likely, in fact, to sell a stock if he hears that it is being recommended and to buy a stock if he hears it is being dumped—especially if the recommended stock is behaving poorly and the stock being dumped is giving ground slowly. He reasons that once the buying pressure resulting from the recommendation dries up, the stock is likely to go down, whereas once the selling pressure eases, the stock is likely to go up. In short, he is constantly interpreting information in terms of the way the market itself acts.

There are many registered representatives who mouth the same philosophy of the market as John Holland. Containing as it does elements from a number of different approaches, this is not surprising. Most of these other brokers, however, are not true Traders, since they don't act in accordance with their "philosophy." John Holland does, and moreover has done so successfully. Starting with relatively no capital, he has amassed a significant portfolio as well as acquired a number of large accounts. He admits that in the earlier days he often traded with an eye to his commissions, but he seldom, if ever, does so today. To begin with, he doesn't need money. Today, he buys and sells for his clients as well as for himself only when he believes that he can make money through capital gains. He not only feels that he can make more money this way; he also needs the constant exposure to the market to keep his feel for it. Commissions are secondary, if still appreciated.

John Holland is not only willing but also eager to test himself and his philosophy against the market. It is this characteristic more than anything else that distinguishes John Holland and other True Believers. All True Believers think that they are right and expect in the long run to be proven right. Some, like Ann Klein, are also interested in testing some theory. John Holland puts himself to the test.

This need to test himself affects what John Holland does. Given his present financial situation, it makes little sense for him to trade on a short-term basis. Nevertheless, he still trades, though admittedly less than when he was younger. Similarly, he is still willing to invest substantial sums of money. If he were to trade only in small sums, he would not be able to experience the tensions and doubts from which he develops his feel for the market. Without this feel, he would seriously consider getting out of the market.

John Holland knows that he's good. Not only does his portfolio speak for itself, but also his professional colleagues shower him with respect and admiration. There is always someone wanting to know how he feels about this or that. As a result, he has managed to develop a network of very good contacts. Even Hank Strong would be pleased to have some of John's contacts. And Holland knows that he is not only good but actually a lot better than most other brokers. Though he freely admits this, he's not as down on other brokers as are Bill Chester or Ann Klein. There are some of whom he is very critical; such feelings are generally reserved for those who he feels take advantage of their customers. The simple ignorance of most brokers he accepts more as a fact of life than as a flaw in their character.

John Holland's attitude toward his customers is similar to his attitude toward brokers. Some of his customers, he feels, have no understanding of the market whatsoever. Others have a degree of sophistication, most of which they have gained from him. He feels few, if any, could survive on their own. When customers begin to "second guess" him, he like to let them go on their own for a while just to teach them a lesson. Usually they fall into line fairly quickly.

Initially, like most young brokers, John Holland had to solicit accounts, but for a number of years, this hasn't been necessary. Most of his new accounts, like those of Bill Chester, come in through referrals. Unlike Bill Chester, however, John Holland is likely to drop an account that becomes too demanding, questions trades, becomes too emotional, or in other ways causes him trouble. This is usually done in such a way that the customer doesn't know what is happening. He is allowed to act more and more on his own and then allowed to drift off. The customer more often than not thinks that he left John Holland.

Being a Trader who relies on his feel for the market, John requires a relatively high degree of discretion in what he does. Few, if any, of his accounts are officially discretionary accounts, but he handles most accounts as if they were. He doesn't buy anything out of the blue for a client and normally limits his purchases to the customer's cash reserve. Similarly, he is likely to give the customer a phone call within minutes of the transaction. There has usually also been some sort of preliminary discussion about the transaction before it occurred. He has, however, little use for lengthy discussions before such executions. He similarly makes little use of the mail.

John Holland may not respect the sophistication of most of his clients, but he does respect their basic attitudes toward the market. He doesn't treat all of his clients the same way. Some customers can afford and are willing to take a high degree of risk; others cannot. He keeps this in mind in managing his various accounts. He admits to being more comfortable with customers who can afford and are willing to trade, but he will not try to trade someone whom he feels should not be trading.

As Bill Chester needs his reports, Hank Strong his information, and Ann Klein her charts, John Holland needs to be in touch with the flow of the market. Until relatively recently, he did this by watching the tape. Today, he is restricted to the quotes that are constantly being updated on his computer screen. He manages to operate this way, but as he has often noted, "It's just not the same." He also needs a firm that can give him good executions. Getting an order to the floor quickly can be the difference between making money and losing money. For this reason, John, unlike most brokers, takes a real interest in what's happening on the floor of the various Exchanges. He takes time regularly to meet and talk to the floor brokers from his firm. Earlier in his career when specialists were given more leeway in how they executed order, he took a great interest in the styles of the different specialists.[37] As a result, he used to be able to tell you if a specialist was taking in shorts just by reading the rhythm of the tape and price differentials. He wasn't always right, but he was right more often than not.

To understand John Holland, it's necessary to remember that he enjoys the market. Bill Chester and Hank Strong are comfortable and at home in the market, and Ann Klein is addicted to it. John Holland delights in it. Simply put, he finds the market to be fun. He loves the sport of it, and last, but not least, he loves winning.

To a large extent, John's enjoyment is due to his own success, but there is clearly more to it than this. Having thought about it for some time, I have reached the conclusion that it's the "game aspect" of the market that turns on John Holland and others like him. Nearly everyone in the market is, to some degree, affected by this quality of the market—they enjoy the excitement and action—but they don't relish it. John Holland gets a kick out of the fickleness of the market even when he gets hurt by it. He loves to see how it twists and turns, starts and stops. He's constantly seeking to learn from it—not merely so that he can be a better trader, but also for a better understanding of life in general. Here I may be pushing things somewhat, but it is a fact that John Holland is always using market analogies to explain a wide range of nonmarket behavior. This is the case for all True Believers, but it has a special intensity with John Holland.

So what makes John Holland tick? We saw that Bill Chester was primarily concerned with underlying economic factors, that Hank Strong was primarily interested in information and market muscle, and that Ann Klein is primarily concerned with the underlying pattern or the hand of God. What is John Holland really concerned with; what does he focus upon? The best answer I can offer is that he's concerned with the lifeblood of the market, its essential energy. One could almost say that he's interested in the market's libido. Given the way he loves and enjoys the market, such a concept is not as extravagant as it may initially appear. What is perhaps equally noteworthy is that after forty years he still finds the market alluring.

All love affairs, however, are apt to change over a forty-year period, and John's love affair with the market is no exception. John has changed; the market has changed. The most significant change for John has been that he has become more conservative as he has gotten older. The losses are more painful than they were when he was younger, and the victories are less exhilarating. This is due in part, he will admit, to changes in his own financial situation. It is also due, however, to the fact that John has less ego involved in his trading. He is a professional who knows how to play by the rules. Sometimes he will lose and sometimes he will win. Whatever happens, however, he no longer feels as if his own ego is on the line.

Whatever changes John has undergone, however, pale in comparison to the changes that the market, or at least John's market, has undergone during the same period. Some of these changes have been noted earlier: the loss of the tape; the dominance of institutional investors; the technological revolution in the market; the exponential growth in information; new products; and the acceleration of basically everything. As we have already seen, these changes have had an impact on nearly everyone. They have had perhaps the greatest impact, however, on Traders like John Holland.

John's expertise rested on not only the way he could sense the underlying currents of the market, but also how he could ride with and exploit these underlying currents. The size and strength of these currents have grown so large in recent years, however—due in large part to the growing role of institutional investors—that even a John Holland finds it difficult and dangerous to attempt to ride the currents. Increased volatility makes it very difficult to use a short-loss strategy. The rapid dissemination of information makes it difficult to get ahead of a move, and the existence of sophisticated computer-based trading programs also makes it difficult to locate trading inefficiencies.

In the eighties and into the late nineties, John attempted to adjust to some of these changes by utilizing options. The two dominant strategies were to seek out inefficiencies and to limit risk. He was relatively successful with a number of different strategies in the earlier years, but the increased sophistication of institutional investors backed up by the tremendous technical capacity rapidly eliminated any edge that he once might have had. More recently, he has tended to revert to the approach he relied upon most when he began in the market in the fifties, namely the selection of the best-acting stocks, preferably in a weak market. As he says, "It's still fun, but it gets tougher every day."

Somewhat ironically, this dramatically increased volatility has also given rise to a new breed of Trader, namely the amateur day Trader. These Traders are normally lay players who have spent on average between $5,000 and $10,000 to take a three-to-five-week course in day trading that is meant to show them how to make money day trading. They have then plunked down between $50,000 to $100,000 to open a day-trading account with one of a relatively small number of firms that cater to this clientele. The idea behind such day trading is quite simple. The trading process entails that major market makers—be they New York Stock Exchange specialists or firms making markets in particular stocks—post bid and ask prices for the stocks they trade. At any given time there is normally a gap of a quarter of a point or more between the bid and the ask prices. That is, the specialist or firm indicates that they will sell a particular stock at $25\frac{1}{2}$ and buy it at $25\frac{1}{4}$. Theoretically this means that a day Trader willing to buy that stock for $25\frac{5}{16}$ could acquire the stock ahead of the professional Trader and then sell it for 25$^{7}/_{16}$, again ahead of the professional Trader, and make a profit of $^{1}/_{8}$. The problem, of course, is being able to both buy and sell at these prices. The day Trader may be able to buy the stock at 25$^{5}/_{16}$, but discover that the bid has dropped to 25$^{1}/_{4}$ before he or she can sell it and may consequently be forced to sell at 25$^{3}/_{16}$, for a $^{1}/_{8}$ loss. Professionals maintain the larger spread between their bid and ask quotes specifically to protect themselves from such market moves.

Unlike John Holland, few of these day Traders rely on their own feel or understanding of the market. The courses they take provide them with various operational rules—they are trained, for example, to scan the various trading boards looking for spreads within which they can trade. Others focus more on locating stocks that seem to be moving up or down so they can jump in and attempt to get a short ride with the movement. The advantage that these day Traders have over other players, including most professionals, is that they are able to trade for minimal commissions. The governing idea is to attempt to make a small profit on numerous trades. If an active day Trader, who makes hundreds of trades within a few hours, is right just 55 out of 100 times, he or she should theoretically be able to make a profit each day.

The last few years have been very kind to many day Traders, especially in the performance of many of the high-multiple technology stocks. Since these stocks have been up many more days than they have been down in recent years, day Traders willing to simply go with the market leaders have done quite well. How well they have done since mid-1998 isn't so clear. My guess is that more than a few are finding the going tougher—as has John Holland.

6

AN EFFICIENT MARKET BELIEVER
AND ENHANCER

As noted in the "Preface," in my first book on the market, I didn't treat believers in the Efficient Market theory as True Believers because they didn't believe that they could beat the market. There have been a number of important developments over the years, however, that have led me now to classify them as True Believers. Perhaps the most important of these developments has been the hard fact that few if any actively managed investment portfolios have outperformed the standard stock market indexes over time. (To put this another way, though index funds have not beaten the market as measured by such indexes—a logical impossibility, since they are structured to mirror such indexes—they have outperformed nearly all other funds. As such, an index strategy can now be said to beat the market provided one measures the market in terms of the performances of other funds rather than market indexes.) This situation has led to a rush toward such funds and the spread of acceptance of this investment philosophy.

This acceptance, however, has generated its own ripples. The success of index funds has led some professional investors to refocus their energies. Rather than attempt to outperform the index through an actively managed portfolio, they have elected to go with an index fund in an attempt to outperform most other funds and then fine tune their index fund to slightly outperform the other index funds by making slight adjustments in the amounts of stock held in different companies based on their own analysis. These are what I have referred to as Efficient Market Enhancers. To properly understand what this entails, however, it is necessary to place such Enhancers in the proper

context. To do this, I now reintroduce Dave Gibbons from my first book.
Though the presentation that follows was originally set in the late seventies,
except for a few minor details it could all have occurred yesterday. Once we
have heard from Dave Gibbons, we will hear a little from a second-generation,
efficient market theorist, who will explain what it means to be an Efficient
Market Enhancer.

Dave Gibbons had been a retail broker, an institutional broker, and an analyst, whom I met in 1980; at that time he was a money manager employed by
the trust department of a relatively small bank. He was in charge of two substantial pension funds and a number of smaller private accounts. He earned a
very good salary, was pleasant and quite polished. In many ways, he came
across as a younger—he was in his early forties—less established, Bill Chester.

This was not surprising, since he claimed for a numbers of years that he was
a young Bill Chester insofar as he shared Bill Chester's view of the market.
Entering the market with a master's in economics, he found the Fundamentalist view most congenial, but became disenchanted with it in the mid-sixties.
While he was buying sound companies for himself and his customers, the "go-
go boys" were making all the money. He soon became convinced that there
was more to the market than fundamentals. He admits that the fact that he
was unable to make a living as a Fundamentalist played a role in his conversion.

He is quick to add, however, that it was more than these financial pressures
that changed his mind. Functioning as a broker, he developed more and more
respect for the technical side of the market. He never adopted the extreme
views of an Ann Klein, but he became convinced that there was something to
be said for a more technical approach. He similarly developed more respect
for the influence of information, though never to the extent of a Hank Strong.

In discussing this period of his career, he characterizes himself as a junior
version of John Holland. For a while he was quite successful; he began to think
he was a pretty good Trader. He focused upon growth companies, followed the
tape closely, and traded freely. Then he took a couple of beatings. When this
happened, like a good Trader, he stepped back to get his bearings. He tried
again and got hurt again. After that, he says he came to the hard conclusion that
he really wasn't meant to be a Trader. It was not that he thought he couldn't do
it if he tried—the period during which he got hurt was an especially difficult
period—but rather that he just was not enjoying it. He wasn't sleeping and his
stomach was constantly upset. "It takes a special type of person to trade in the
market. I'm just not that type."

When pressed on the matter, he expressed the opinion that there are only a few people who, for a combination of reasons, can trade successfully over the long haul. Consequently, it was not a sensible approach for most, including him.

As a result of these various experiences, Dave Gibbons concluded that there is no way for most people to beat the market. This does not mean that he believed people should not be in the market. To quote: "A significant proportion of assets belong in the market; stocks are still the best protection against inflation. Moreover, stocks are bound to move higher as the economy grows. You cannot beat the market, however, because the market at any time is the best indicator of its own true value. You can't beat the market because it responds too quickly to all significant information. By the time you hear or see anything, be it information on earnings, the decision of a large fund, a technical breakout, etc., the market has already discounted it." To use the market jargon of today, Dave Gibbons became a convert to the Efficient Market theory.[38]

The conclusion put Dave Gibbons in an awkward position. Here he was, a self-proclaimed market expert who believed that he couldn't beat the market. He soon found out that he wasn't alone. True, not many brokers or money managers felt this way, or at least were willing to admit it publicly, but there was a sizable number of people with substantial sums of money who did. Among his own accounts, he found two persons who had reached the same conclusion. Whatever reservations he had were finally put to rest with the emergence from the academic world of the Efficient Market theory.

Dave Gibbons constructed what could be called a semi-index fund; that is, his investments were, by and large, a mirror image of the market as a whole. He did not go so far as to invest a little bit of money in every company; he did not think it was necessary, nor did he have the resources, so he tended to stick with major companies. He tried, however, to avoid weighting his investment in any direction. He didn't want to beat the market; he just didn't want to be beaten by it. The only real flexibility he allowed himself was the amount of money he had in the market. He always maintained 50 percent in the market and 30 percent in the equivalent of treasuries; the other 20 percent could be either in stocks or treasuries, depending on his general feel for the market as a whole.

As an early convert, Dave Gibbons for years kept a low profile. At that time, the bank for which he worked did not favor the Efficient Market theory, and their official line was that they could beat the market. Some of his clients, too, still wanted to beat the market. Fortunately, he worked for a fairly conservative bank, and most of his clients tended to be conservative. He was able, therefore, to justify his investments in terms of diversification for safety. Nevertheless, he believed that most of his clients, as well as most of his co-workers, knew what he was doing. Since he had done pretty well, especially in contrast to most other money managers, no one complained. Moreover, he believed that in the future his view of the market would become more respectable among market professionals.

Dave Gibbons's opinion of almost everyone associated with the market was influenced by his view of the market. He was not as down on the small investor, for example, as were most market professionals. He agreed with other professionals that the small investor cannot beat the market, but in this respect he judged the small investor to be no different from anyone else. He was irked only by the small investor who was greedy, or who expected to make an easy fortune in the market.

It was the professionals who really bothered him, because as far as Dave Gibbons was concerned, they should have known better. It was this notion that distinguished Dave Gibbons's from the general low opinion that most professionals have of each other: They claim that most professionals are out for themselves and are lazy. (They may also complain that others don't understand the market, but this is usually secondary.) Few expect to be students of the market, and it is specifically this lack of understanding that most upset Dave Gibbons. "There simply isn't that much to understand. The problem isn't that they don't understand the economics of the market, the importance of information, market cycles, or the dynamic of the market, but rather that they will not admit that they can't beat the market."

Most market professionals took a dim view of the Efficient Market theory twenty years ago, yet even then it had a seductive quality. If failing to outperform the market was not the fault of the broker, analyst, or money manager, then a person couldn't really be held responsible. There is something very reassuring about this. As a consequence, even among those who most vociferously attacked the view, there was a good number who secretly fancied it. As fewer and fewer money managers were able to outperform the index, these numbers grew, especially among large institutional investors. Twenty years ago, Dave had to keep a low profile, but today he is clearly mainstream. Though few believers in the Efficient Market theory were likely to spread the gospel twenty years ago, today they are treated as prophets of great wisdom.

It has been this very success of the Efficient Market theory, ironically, that has given rise to its mutated, "enhanced" version. To understand this new form, we need to talk with a second-generation Efficient Market theorist—someone who grew up in a market where the efficient theory was already accepted and where the task was to find ways of "improving" it. Dave Green is such a person.

Dave Green's background is quite different from that of Dave Gibbons. His educational background was both more intense and more theoretical. He has a Ph.D. in mathematics and has taught at the college level for a number of years. Even today, after nearly two decades in the market and an income that he couldn't have even dreamed about as an academic, he looks, sounds, and acts more like a professor than a money manager. This is perhaps not that surprising given that, in many ways, his move into the market was accidental. Worried about his future as an academic during the cutbacks in the seventies, he elected to explore some nonacademic positions. One thing led to another, and within a year or so he was hired as a technical analyst by a very large mutual fund to advise them on their proprietary technical trading programs, which utilized fairly sophisticated mathematical modeling.

Though Dave Green was familiar with the market before making his move, like most new initiates, he did not have any real market philosophy. Whereas Dave Gibbons came to the Efficient Market theory basically on his own and only slowly, Dave Green had it handed to him. By the mid-eighties the Efficient Market theory was the dominant perspective, or minimally one of the major perspectives, of the company for which he worked. (For a large mutual fund, an index fund generated by the Efficient Market theory has the advantage of requiring less turnover than an actively managed fund, which not only saves commissions but also makes it easier to manage very large sums of money.) His own readings and the performance of the market since his arrival on Wall Street have only served to solidify his confidence in the general soundness of the view.

Although the Efficient Market theory was highly respected within the firm, the firm—like nearly all large mutual fund managers—ran a range of different types of funds, including a number of actively managed funds. This required that the firm maintain its own research and analysis capabilities and continue to engage in stock selection. The task given to Dave Green and his team was to find ways to utilize these resources within the context of what was basically an index fund. As mathematicians, mathematically inclined economists, and computer programmers, the team's approach was to generate algorithms—basically, complex investment strategies—that would maximize return on investment. They did this by working out various investment strategies and then seeing how these strategies would have worked during earlier markets. Given the comparative success of index funds over actively managed funds, coupled with the requirement that any strategy be capable of managing billions of dollars, the team limited itself to strategies heavily dependent upon an Efficient Market approach. The objective was to see to what extent the stocks in a broad-based index fund could be overweighted and underweighted to outperform the underlying index while maintaining the basic pattern of the index. They were also interested in determining what rate of portfolio turnover maximized return over the years. Other programs were generated to determine how the size and rhythm of trading affected return on investment. As a very large investor, it was important for the firm to determine the various ways the fund's own actions of buying and selling stocks affected the price of those stocks. Here the problem was to find out just how much and how fast stock could be acquired and dispersed without creating negative repercussions.

Each of these different objectives led to a particular investment strategy, which then had to be integrated with the others to form an overall strategy. This general strategy, in turn, had to be constantly updated based upon how the market behaved. The final result was what the street now refers to as enhanced indexing. A number of mutual and pension funds now run a sizable portion of their funds in this manner. Each organization has its own particular proprietary program based upon how the fund weights numerous factors and the extent to which it is willing to deviate from the portfolio dictated by the underlying index. Funds also differ in the specific index they select as a yardstick, be it the S&P 500, the Dow, the Russell 2000, the Russell 3000 or any other index. Finally, in a throwback to the heyday of Dave Gibbons, they also differ to the extent to which they are willing to admit that they are indexing in any way.

The Efficient Market theory may not be right, but it is simple, and there is something very attractive about a simple theory. In light of this fact, I asked Dave Green the same question I had asked Dave Gibbons nearly twenty years earlier: "What would happen if everyone, or minimally most large institutional investors, adopted an index approach to the market? Wouldn't that create conditions that would negate its own validity? If everyone put their money in an index fund, wouldn't the market cease to adapt to new information?" "That's the beauty about enhanced indexing," he answered with a smile. "We can still respond to changes. The fact that we manage so much money means that, even though from a percentage point of view we can only respond in a small way, the net effect can be sizable. Moreover, if a number of other large institutional investors is doing the same thing, especially when combined with the action of traders and active managers, there would be more than enough selling and buying to keep the market basically efficient. In fact, if anything, I am more concerned that the market will become more efficient and hence volatility will increase. This is all speculation, however. Only time will tell what will happen, and then there will be people like me constantly recalibrating what we do so that there will be new offsetting pressures at work. The market may be pretty efficient, but that doesn't mean that it doesn't change."

I should note before concluding this chapter that some market observers aren't as complacent as Dave Green about the dangers inherent in this rush toward index funds, especially index funds built around the Dow Jones Index and the S&P Index, in contrast to the Russell Index that Dave Green uses. These critics fear that major, increased investment in these more limited index funds will lead to an overvaluation of their underlying stocks. If this happens, these critics fear that a correction will become inevitable, and when that happens not only will many investors be hurt but also there will be forced selling leading to a potentially very destructive sell-off in the key stocks that make up these major indexes.

7

A TRANSFORMATIONAL
IDEA ADHERENT

Sarah Wright represents a new breed of True Believer. It is not so much the substance of her belief—the market responds to and is governed by original and exciting ideas—that is new, but rather her complete commitment to this idea. As we have already seen, most other True Believers—Fundamentalists, Insiders, and Traders—weight heavily ideas and good stories. Fundamentalists, however, are interested in how such ideas and stories affect the fortunes of different companies; Insiders are interested in how they affect the buying and selling of major players; and Traders are concerned with how they affect market action. Sarah Wright is attentive to evaluating the ideas and stories in and of themselves. Her position is that both good and bad ideas and stories will have effects that will eventually motivate the Fundamentalists, Insiders, and Traders, but that by acting on the ideas and stories directly, she can get a jump on all of them.

Despite growing up with the market—her father is a very successful institutional broker for a major Wall Street firm—she never thought that she would end up there. She graduated from a prestigious Ivy League college with a major in English. After traveling for a year, she floated into advertising, writing copy for a number of the agency's smaller accounts. Many of these companies were new technology companies in computer software, the Internet, and health care. As she came to know these companies in greater detail—part of her job required going through company statements and projections—she became more and more fascinated. As she watched the stocks of some of them rise, she became more than fascinated: She became excited.

She didn't do much more than observe what was going on, however, for some time. Her father played a significant role in her hesitancy to act. She had discussed a number of these companies with her father from almost the moment that she had become intrigued by them. His advice was to avoid them. Given that he was basically a Fundamentalist, this was not surprising. Each new explosive move, however, caused Sarah to question her father's judgment and the assumptions upon which it was based. She began to read more broadly in market-related periodicals and investment guides. What she found was that, although the great majority of so-called experts were in agreement with her father, others favored a much more radical approach. In effect, what they claimed was that the best returns on your money came from the high-flying, future-oriented companies like the technology companies that she had been following. These other experts argued that you shouldn't pick your stocks in terms of where the company was today, but where it was likely to be in five to ten years. You invest for the future, so you should be looking to the future. Don't worry about what a company might be earning today or even the type of institutional support it presently has. Focus on where it will be tomorrow.

Encouraged by this new view of the market, Sarah began to play the market with the little nest egg she had put together over the years. The times were right, her selections were on target, and she was very, very successful. Within eighteen months she had tripled her initial investment capital. Shortly afterwards she made the leap to Wall Street. Through a connection that her father provided, she took a position with a start-up hedge fund, which focused on high-tech companies of the type that Sarah had been following. It was a small fund that allowed her to engage in both sales and analysis. Her workdays have lengthened considerably and she has also had to do a fair amount of traveling, but it has all been worth it. She is now paid three to four times what she was earning previously, her own investments continue to do well, and, most importantly, she claims to be enjoying almost every minute of it.

Sarah also looks like she is enjoying it. It is not that she has changed in any obvious way. She dresses very much the way she always has—in expensive, understated suits and dresses. Having more money gives her some added economic freedom, but she always had more than enough money to do what she wanted to do. The difference is that now it is money that she has acquired rather than money acquired by grandparents, parents, or other relatives. And, it is money that she has amassed by following her own instincts and strategy rather than by doing what she was told to do. In fact, what probably gives her more pleasure than anything else is the fact that she has even convinced her father to take a fly on some of her more speculative ideas—and he has made money. Admittedly, he still continues to preach a more Fundamentalist philosophy to her, but he doesn't hide the fact that he is quite proud of what she has been able to do.

So what is this strategy, and how does it compare to and differ from those of the other True Believers we have met? As mentioned earlier, Sarah is not the only person to look for a good story; Fundamentalists, Insiders, and Traders are all interested in them. She is also not the only one to favor glamour stocks; both Insiders and Traders tend to favor such stocks. She isn't even the first person to argue that one can pretty much ignore everything but the story. Though not true of Insiders and Traders, many of the gunslingers of the sixties would go on a story as easily as Sarah does. She differs somewhat from her earlier reincarnations in her strategies for coming up with stories and ideas. She doesn't give much weight to Wall Street rumors, or for that matter to Wall Street wisdom. She is much more likely to seek out her leads in trade magazines and in talking to people, especially the younger ones, working in the high-tech industries that she follows most closely. In this respect, she is actually quite like her father and other Fundamentalists, but she differs in the types of information she seeks. Whereas Fundamentalists focus on earnings, sales, and other economic factors, Sarah is more interested in big-picture issues. How do the high-tech experts envision the future? Will we all, for example, be walking around with high-powered minicomputers, or will we rather be connected by an infrared network to multiple servers? Will we attempt to eliminate disease by coming up with new drugs capable of controlling specific viruses and bacteria, or are we more likely to attempt to discover ways to make us more immune to such agents? In short, Sarah isn't so much interested in stories that offer opportunities within the market as she is in stories that promise to transform the way we live. These developments will have a profound impact eventually on the market, or minimally some aspect of the market. As such, she should perhaps be called a true dreamer rather than a True Believer, but then all True Believers might be categorized as dreamers. So far her dreams have been happy dreams.

These happy dreams are not surprising in light of the explosive market that Sarah has ridden. Nearly everything that she has ever bought has gone up and then continued to go up. She was in the market during the 1992 correction, but she claims that she always believed that it was only a correction and used the sell-off as an opportunity to buy. She responded the same way to the sell-off in 1998. It is too early to tell yet whether she will be proven correct again, or whether she will be forced to absorb some serious losses. Personally, she is unlikely to get hurt, since most of her holdings were bought at much lower prices and she hasn't ever made use of margin buying (a bit of advice from her father she still follows). However, the hard reality is that she hasn't yet ever been in a real, long-term, bear market. One can't consequently predict whether such a bear market will force her to change her views.

I raise this question because, although I have labeled Sarah a True Believer, I have my doubts as to the depth of her convictions. All the other True Believers we have met—and the types they represent—have been in the market for some time in up markets and in down markets. They have all been tested. Sarah has yet to be seriously tested. In the sixties and at other times, there have been those whose views were very similar to those of Sarah but who faded when the market faded. Already there has been some erosion in what might be called the purity of her position. Though she claims that it is the basic story and vision that determine what she does, she is not loath to include other types of information bearing on such things as earnings, institutional backings, and market performance to convince clients to accept her recommendations. It is quite possible, especially if the market turns downwards or even sideways for a period of time, that she will herself begin to weigh these factors more heavily. Only time will tell.

Sarah—and her ilk—may be only a flash in the pan, but she may also represent something more. Put quite simply, Sarah treats stories qualitatively differently from other players in the market. It is this difference that tempts me to call her a market postmodernist. Like postmodernists found elsewhere, Sarah doesn't accept the view that there is a nuts-and-bolts reality out there that determines what will be. Obviously, there is something out there, but what will be is determined primarily by the way we frame what is. Virtual reality and reality are part of the same continuum. Though we can't transform every image into a reality, potent images do have transforming power. In taking this position, Sarah elevates knowledge to a different level from that commonly given it on Wall Street. All True Believers treat knowledge as fundamental, though they clearly differ as to the types of knowledge they see as most basic. Only Sarah endows knowledge with Transformational powers. This is an issue to which we will return later. For now, however, I am willing to accept her as a new type of True Believer.

Although all True Believers are convinced that their view of the market is the correct view, all are equally convinced that their views are bound to remain minority views. In the beginning, I found this somewhat strange, but later it began to make sense to me; furthermore, it shed new light upon the True Believers of the market.

The True Believers could be called the priests of the market insofar as they are spokespersons for the major market "religions." The market, however, is a very secular place. True Believers consequently are more likely to see themselves as prophets than priests; like the prophets of old, they see themselves as living among "pagans." Without the pagans, they would not be True Believers.

Do all True Believers favor either the Fundamentalist, Insider, Cyclist-Chartist, Trader, Efficient Market, or Transformational Idea view? Are there no other types? Can the types be mixed?

Probably the most central of these questions is the last, since it directly bears on the first two. To some extent, the various types could be mixed. In fact, we saw that Bill Chester, Hank Strong, Ann Klein, John Holland, Dave Gibbons, Dave Green, and Sarah Wright all exhibited some sympathy for certain aspects of each other's views. However, they really do not incorporate these aspects into their own views. It would seem that one can't do this and still maintain the ideological purity required of True Believers. A salesman, yes; a True Believer, no. The ideological tensions seem to be too great. I ran into a number of people with their own peculiar view of the market, but I did not discover another view that had the scope or was as consistent as the six views presented above.

This is really not surprising, since, as indicated earlier, these overviews reflect the basic intentional dimensions that we use in defining any and all social situations. If I had discovered another basic overview, I would have seriously had to question my assumptions regarding the intentional dimensions.

Though True Believers tend to be loyal to a single view whatever the view might be, these overviews become intertwined in the public domain. This creates an ironic situation, namely, that more makes for less. More concretely, though each overview seeks to impose some sort of order and sensibility upon the market—and in fact does so quite nicely—each becomes a source of added confusion when it is joined with another overview, because each defines the market differently. Even when True Believers of differing orientations agree with each other (for example, on buying or selling a specific stock), they normally do so for completely different reasons.

For any True Believers, such ambiguities and conflicts are of little or no importance. A True Believer has a proprietary vision of the market and is seldom bothered or concerned with those whose views differ. It is rather the nonbelievers who suffer from these contradictions; it is the nonbeliever who tries to navigate a path between and among the different overviews. One might ask why one would even bother. The answer is that there is no other choice. Even persons who feel and claim that they are not interested in the theoretical concerns of the True Believers are caught in the definitions of the market the True Believers put forth.

PART III

SELLING THE MARKET

8

THE HARD FACTS OF MARKET LIFE

Most market professionals are not True Believers; they have neither the aptitude nor the inclination. More importantly, they cannot afford to be, because though they often feign to be students of the market, they are first and foremost salesmen; they make their living selling stocks. This is a fact of market life. It is inherent in the very structure of the market.

Brokers are paid on a commission basis. For every sale they make—transaction they execute—they are paid a fee. The fee is derived from the commission paid by their customers; the actual fee varies from broker to broker. Some receive 25 percent of the gross commission, others earn up to 50 percent. This is true even of those brokers who are apparently salaried. In such cases, the broker may have to wait till bonus time before his account is straightened out. Admittedly, it does not always work out exactly, but all brokers realize that what they take home is directly determined by the commissions they generate.[39]

To a lesser degree, the same holds true for analysts and money managers, though their earnings may be determined more by the sums they manage than by the amount of business they are able to generate. Since a number of people usually work on the same large institutional account, it is also more difficult to determine who deserves credit for any specific order; this is especially the case with analysts. Nevertheless, the general relationship holds. Sales generate income.

Brokerage firms earn their income through commissions, trading and investments, interest from cash in customer's accounts, interest on margin debt, and numerous other sources.[40] This is how the market works. Recently, some firms have been attempting to replace their commission income by charging a set annual management fee. These accounts are commonly referred to as wrap accounts because all charges are wrapped together in the basic fee charged. In some cases—generally discretionary accounts—there may be a management fee plus a transaction cost agreement. Whatever the specific arrangement, everyone knows that in most cases the greater the number of transactions, the greater the income. They similarly know that the more business generated, the greater the rewards to the individual broker or money manager.

It is not surprising, therefore, that most market professionals see their job primarily as soliciting and executing market orders. This situation puts most brokers in a difficult position. On the one hand, they are supposed to give expert advice to their customers; and on the other, they have to generate business. For those who have the ability to give expert advice, this situation does not create great difficulty. Market expertise is one of the best sales tools that a broker has;[41] most brokers, unfortunately, do not possess it. In fact, what expertise they have more often than not serves to make them cautious rather than aggressive. It is easier to recognize the dangers inherent in an investment than to pick a stock that is likely to double. As a consequence, whatever expertise the average broker has may actually hinder him or her from aggressively soliciting orders.

Most brokers know this. So though all brokers consider themselves to be market professionals, few consider themselves to be market experts; among those few, fewer are, in fact, experts. Most will freely admit that they are salesmen, not stock analysts. Their job is to sell stocks. They try, of course, to sell stocks that will appreciate in value, and if the stocks they recommend do well, it is easier to make future sales. The solicitation of orders is the main objective, however, not picking market winners.

A broker is more than a salesman. One can't simply walk into a Wall Street firm and expect to be able to function as a broker; the market is governed by a wide range of rules and regulations.[42] There are numerous types of orders, such as held and not-held orders, limit orders, market orders, day orders and such. There are also options, short sales, "box" sales, and seemingless countless others. A broker has to know how to execute all of these orders—what forms to fill out and how to fill them out. Furthermore, a broker has to know what releases are required from customers and the types of securities necessary in each situation. In short, a broker has to be a fairly sophisticated functionary.

In some firms, there is the added pressure to move specific stocks. This is more likely in firms that do a lot of underwriting (they acquire large blocks of stocks for dispersion to their customers). It is generally the small producers who are most exposed to such pressures, though a number of substantial producers also engage in this type of operation.

Most customers are aware of these pressures—if anything, they overestimate their importance, believing that their broker will push anything his or her firm tells him or her to push. In contrast, market professionals tend to downplay them, and many will go so far as to deny them. But they cannot deny that it is specifically in terms of these factors that the market defines itself. Every year a list of the ten "best" brokers is compiled by a Wall Street trade magazine. What are the criteria used in establishing this list? Those brokers who best predicted what the market would do? Those brokers who picked the most outstanding stocks during the last year? Those brokers who made the most money for their clients? Those brokers who best outperformed the market as a whole? Those brokers judged by their colleagues to understand the market best? Those brokers judged by their customers to be the most considerate and helpful? The answer to all of these questions is no. The "best broker" list is determined primarily by the amount of commission business generated.[43]

Within firms, another process is at work. The so-called best brokers are clearly those who produce, but a modest producer who goes by the book and whose orders are always in the proper form will generally be judged a "good" broker. A modest producer who continually makes bureaucratic mistakes, however, whatever his market expertise, is likely to be out on the street. Such a broker is too dangerous to keep around. He can expose a firm to all sorts of suits and sanctions.

This explains why so few brokers, money managers, or even analysts become True Believers. There is simply no profit in it. It would be wrong, however, to conclude that the average broker, money manager, or analyst has no interest in the views of the True Believer. Whatever their personal understanding or lack of understanding and whatever their personal bias toward theoretical models in general, market professionals cannot ignore the general overviews of the market, since their customers and their clients expect them to have an integrated overview of the market. Whether they like it or not, therefore, they are forced to simulate some sort of ideological commitment.

Most, especially the retail broker, will simulate whatever beliefs work best in soliciting orders, using whatever ideology or credo seems most appropriate at the time. Sometimes they will focus upon earnings and other sorts of economic fundamentals; at other times, they will stress a story or some sort of "inside" information; at other times, they will refer to technical factors; and at yet other times, they will rely upon their own feel for the market. The particular mix will be influenced by the firm for which they work, the biases of their customers, where the market is at the time, their most recent experiences, who they talk to, or any other of a host of factors.

This may make it appear as if all, or most, brokers are phonies. Such a judgment is really not fair. The average broker who behaves in this way more often than not is fully convinced of what he or she is saying. Few deliberately try to mislead. The problem is that brokers have no strong opinion as to what's going on or what makes the market work. They listen to what others have to say and are convinced by this argument or that one in much the same way as their customers. More often than not, it's a simple case of the blind leading the blind.

There are other factors that influence the particular stance that a broker, money manager, or analyst will take at any time. Nearly all brokerage firms provide their salesmen with recommendations. Besides pushing specific stocks, these recommendations usually push one view of the market: Most firms' recommendations rely heavily on economic factors; some make use of technical factors. Customers, too, vary in the types of companies they want to own: Some want to maximize safety, others want to maximize capital gains. A salesperson is primarily concerned with sales and is normally going with what he or she has.

There are good reasons for going along with one's firm or one's customers. In both cases, there is protection if the stock doesn't work out. In the case of a firm's recommendation, the broker can always fall back on the follow-up "explanations" that the firm will no doubt put out. In the second case, the broker can always remind the customer that it was the customer's choice as well as the broker's. Obviously, in neither case is the customer likely to be happy, but neither is the broker likely to be the sole villain.

Going along with the opinion of others affords some protection from abuse, but it also makes it more difficult to acquire true expertise. You become a follower, not a leader. You are too concerned with the views of others, which are themselves often inconsistent, to develop your own view. This doesn't necessarily mean that such brokers cannot do a reasonable job for their customers. It does mean that they are dependent upon the sophistication of their firm and/or their customers. In this respect, the sales broker is quite different from the True Believer, who leads rather than follows.

Some salespersons—those who work for the larger firms with a great deal of in-house research—can operate almost exclusively in this passive manner; most cannot. Even the best firms make "bad" recommendations, and even the most sophisticated customers can react irrationally. Most brokers, if they are to survive, must develop some sort of discrimination, though it will be different from the discrimination required of True Believers. The True Believers will stay with those stocks that conform to their own view of the market, and are concerned with picking stocks that they believe will outperform the market. The salesperson has another concern: to pick stocks that customers can live with.

These two types of discrimination are not unrelated. If salespersons feel that a particular stock will not work out, they are not likely to recommend it. On the other hand, most brokers live in dread of knocking a stock and thereby thwarting a sale only to see the stock double. The difficulty is to know when a stock should not be recommended regardless of its future action.

What would constitute such a situation? When the broker is likely to end up out on a limb. This is apt to happen when a customer is tempted to buy a stock unlike those normally bought, or when the firm is recommending a company unlike those it normally recommends. In such situations, if things go wrong, the broker is likely to be accused of putting the customer into a bad situation, and if it was a firm recommendation, there may be no follow-up "explanation." To avoid such situations, a good salesperson must understand customers and how the firm operates—must known when a customer is following a mere whim and when the firm is pushing a stock. This requires more psychological and political expertise than market expertise.

Even those who attempt to survive by psyching out their customers and playing firm politics must know the rhetoric of the market. They don't have to become True Believers, but they must be able to project such an image, even if it is a very eclectic image. Whatever other talents brokers might have, they cannot hope to generate customers' confidence nor to become part of the market establishment without such an image. For most brokers, this is not a difficult task, since they acquire the rhetoric and credos of the market by osmosis.

Salespersons, almost by definition, are not wedded to one approach. They can and do change their "line." Such a change may be due to a switch in firms, exposure to a new service, securing a new contact, or acquiring some new accounts. Or it may be due to no more than some hard times with an old approach. Despite such constant changes, most salespersons at any one time favor one approach over the others. It simply creates less strain.

A broker could come up with his or her own reasons for buying a particular stock at a particular time—astrological signs, mother's intuition, the market symbol of the company—but it is doubtful that customers would accept such reasons. It is also doubtful that any reputable firm would allow a broker to make such recommendations for any length of time. Brokerage firms prefer their salespersons to rely on orthodox reasoning, which means, at least in form, the reasoning of True Believers. This is a fact of market life to which even the most opportunistic salesperson must adjust.

Other factors constrain salespersons to favor one or another of the general views of the market. There is an affinity among the different sales approaches and the different overviews of the market. This was alluded to above, when it was noted that most firm recommendations tend to have a Fundamentalist bias. To make obvious how and why this is so requires a few words of clarification.

In analyzing True Believers, each type was shown to conceive of the market in a different way. Fundamentalists see the market in basically economic terms; Insiders, in interpersonal terms (who is buying, who is selling); Cyclist-Chartists, in terms of some sort of underlying or transcendent order; Traders, in terms of the "life forces and action" of the market itself; Efficient Market adherents, in terms of the inherent efficiency of the market; and Transformational Idea adherents, in terms of revolutionary concepts and ideas. A somewhat analogous process characterizes the way most salespersons look at sales. Twenty years ago when I discussed only four types of True Believers— Fundamentalists, Insiders, Cyclist-Chartists, and Traders—I suggested four matching types of salespersons: (1) pseudo-Fundamentalists, who see sales primarily in economic terms and their task as providing economically attractive products; (2) pseudo-Insiders, who see sales primarily in interpersonal terms and their task as convincing customers to make purchases; (3) pseudo-Cyclist-Chartists, who see sales as part of an ongoing orderly process and their task as matching buyers and sellers; and (4) pseudo-Traders, who see sales primarily in what I can only call libidinal terms and their task as satisfying specific emotive needs. The addition of two new types of True Believers doesn't change matters that drastically, since the views of Efficient Market and Transformational Idea adherents lend themselves to incorporation. More specifically, the Efficient Market theory fits quite nicely into the sales pitch of both the pseudo-Fundamentalist and the pseudo-Cyclist-Chartists; the Transformational Idea approach fits equally well with the pseudo-Insider and pseudo-Trader orientations. The key objective of all salespersons, of course, is to convince customers that a significant percentage of their resources belongs in the market. With these points in mind, it is time to take a closer look at how these salespersons attempt to sell the market. Though each of these types has changed somewhat over the years, the most interesting thing is by how little. I have consequently relied quite heavily upon the basic characterizations that I developed in my earlier book but have added a postscript to each account highlighting what I see to have been the most notable changes.

9

SELLING COMPANIES AND OTHER
FINANCIAL PRODUCTS

The most common type of retail broker is what I call the Firm Salesman.[44] It is not difficult to figure out why. All brokers are paid to sell stocks; it doesn't matter if they are selling stocks to customers or selling the stocks of customers; the end results are the same. But it is not easy to sell stocks; a stock has to be packaged like any other merchandise. As the Madison Avenue saying goes, people buy the sizzle, not the steak.

True Believers like to do their own packaging—that is, they provide their own reasons for buying or selling a particular stock at a particular time. But most brokers have neither the ability nor the interest to do this. They have to get their packaging material from someone else, and most use that provided by their firm. It is readily available, there is always plenty of it, and, whatever its limitations, it usually looks good.

Firm recommendations are also relatively safe. If the stock doesn't work out, the broker can be assured that in most cases his firm will provide him with a reasonable explanation of what went wrong. Furthermore, since other brokers will have been recommending the same stock, neither the broker nor his customers will have to suffer alone. This does not negate the pain that accompanies market losses, but it does tend to assuage it a little, for nowhere does the aphorism "Misery loves company" hold truer than in the market.

By using firm recommendations, a broker can cultivate an image of himself as a "team player." Such an image can have positive payoff. First, it tends to soothe management; they know that you are not about to rock the boat by recommending stocks of which they disapprove, or knock the stocks they recommend. Second, by recommending the stocks recommended by the firm, the broker is doing his bit to prove the firm right. If the brokers working for a particular firm can generate a demand for a stock recommended by the firm, that stock is likely to do well, at least in the short run. Management knows this and has ways of showing its appreciation. This is especially the case if management is involved in underwriting.

A firm can push a stock for any reason it chooses. Most firms, however, with sizable in-house research favor a Fundamentalist approach. Their reasons for doing so are similar to the reasons why most brokers use firm recommendations. To begin with, by projecting a Fundamentalist image, both the firm and the broker can present themselves as down-to-earth, no-nonsense financial advisers; they are dealing with economic "reality." This tends to generate a sense of trust in both the broker and the wares that he is selling. It also allows the broker to "cool out" his customers if the stock recommended does not do well, since he can continue to remind his customers that the stock has "true" value regardless of what its price is at the moment.

The Fundamentalist approach also insures that the firm will always have new stocks to recommend. It is easier to have a slew of in-house analysts looking for fundamentally "undervalued" situations than to have them find companies that should be bought for other reasons, though most firms will include such other reasons if they are available. During the last few years, most firms have begun to rely more heavily on technical factors. With few exceptions, however, the heart of most recommendations remains fundamentally oriented. As a result, most Firm Salesmen can be said to favor, or at least to appear to favor, the Fundamentalist credo.

How does this all work in the broker's day-to-day operations? First, he can expect to find on his desk almost daily the latest research reports put out by his firm. These reports are worth at least a few telephone calls to customers who have in the past indicated some interest in the company or industry recommended. The more aggressive the salesman, the more calls. A synopsis of the report, usually also provided by the firm, may also be included in a general mailing to prospective customers selected by the broker. Such mailings are one of the most distinguishing marks of Firm Salesmen. The more established Firm Salesmen use them less than do the less established, but they still use them.

Firm Salesmen are not generally high-pressure salesmen. They have a product to sell, and they try to sell it, but because of the nature of their product they don't have to push any particular item. If the customer doesn't like one item, there will always be another. In fact, if the Firm Salesman is too aggressive, he tends to work against his own image. He is not in the business of recommending "hot" items but of recommending sound investments. If a customer wants to think it over for a few days, it is perfectly all right. The stock will probably be just as good a value next week as it is today.

Firm Salesmen are strongest, however, when they are on the receiving end—that is, when they are asked about a specific stock by one of their customers. In such situations, they are able to check out the stock with their research departments—the larger firms have an official position on most regularly traded stocks. By making one or two in-house calls, the broker can come back to his customer with a comprehensive evaluation of the situation. More than once I have seen such brokers receive an inquiry regarding a stock about which they knew nothing, and then return the call within a few minutes sounding as if they have followed it all their lives.

This last point touches on an important development over the last two decades, namely, that though most Firm Salesmen still favor the Fundamentalist rhetoric stressed by most firms, they also rely upon the technical rhetoric that most firms now provide. This does not contradict what was said earlier about the Fundamentalist bias of most Firm Salesmen, if one remembers that they are only pseudo-Fundamentalists. When such technical information comes from a respectable firm, it is no longer simply technical information but rather part of a general recommendation of an established firm. One could say that by being filtered through an established firm, technical information is transformed into fundamental information.

When one compares Firm Salesmen with true Fundamentalists—men like Bill Chester—a number of other differences emerges. The Firm Salesman is, for all practical purposes, completely dependent upon his firm's research; he seldom does any of his own. The true Fundamentalist, in contrast, relies on his own research. Even when he likes a particular piece of research done by others, he will check it out for himself. This generates very different attitudes toward firm research.

When asked to judge the value and importance of his own firm's research, the Firm Salesman will nearly always say "very important." He is, furthermore, likely to tout highly the quality of this research. He is also likely to indicate respect for the research of other firms, though this will vary from house to house. (Brokers working for the larger firms with extensive in-house research tend to be more chauvinistic toward their own research than those working for smaller firms.) The true Fundamentalist, in contrast, is apt to be very critical of most in-house research. As far as he is concerned, most such research is written with the sole purpose of pushing some stock and is superficial at best. Though he may respect some institutional research, he's quick to point out that most good research is seldom available to the average broker or his customers.

There are other differences. The true Fundamentalist tends to put his people into a few stocks in which he believes, but most Firm Salesmen favor more diversified portfolios, even to the point of, in recent years, including some of the rhetoric of the Efficient Market adherents. Whereas a true Fundamentalist will continue to acquire stock in the few companies he likes as long as they are within his buying range, a Firm Salesman is always coming up with new situations. The true Fundamentalist is much more likely to stay with his choices over a period of time; he is apt to sell them only if they appreciate to a point where he feels they are fully valued or if there is some basic economic change. The Firm Salesman moves his people in and out of situations to insure that they have the resources to "take advantage" of the next "opportunity" his firm is likely to offer.

The ways true Fundamentalists and Firm Salesmen look at and treat their customers also differ. Firm Salesmen on the surface appear to respect their customers more. They are more likely to go along with their customers' judgments than the true Fundamentalist. In part, this is because they are interested in making sales; customers are usually willing to follow their own hunches. The true Fundamentalist seldom will go along with his customer's ideas.

This does not mean that Firm Salesmen think their customers know what they are doing. They have no more respect for their customers' market judgment than do true Fundamentalists. It's just that they are not as ready to say so publicly, at least not to their customers.

There is an additional factor worth noting in this regard. Both the Firm Salesman and the true Fundamentalist are more likely to respect the opinions of their wealthier customers. For Firm Salesmen, it is the customer's wealth per se that generates respect. Again and again, when asked which customers are the most sophisticated, they answer those with substantial financial resources, period. The true Fundamentalist, in contrast, is not impressed by his customers' financial resources; he is impressed by the economic information such customers are likely to have. He does not listen to them for their market judgment but for the specific business information they may offer.

Above, I stated that the Firm Salesman only "appears" to respect his customers more. I stressed the notion of appearance, because it can be argued that the true Fundamentalist exhibits more genuine respect. The true Fundamentalist is more aware that he is playing with other people's money. He may respect their market judgment less, but his concern for their general financial situation is greater. The true Fundamentalist is also more likely to explain his customers' lack of market sophistication in terms of the time required to understand the market than in terms of their lack of intelligence or their greed. He tends to see himself much more as a teacher and guide than does a Firm Salesman, and since he is less likely to execute the hunches of his customers, the Fundamentalist is more likely to explain his reasoning. And since the true Fundamentalist generally has more discretionary control over his accounts than does a Firm Salesman, it is more important that the true Fundamentalist's customers understand why he has acted as he has.

The true Fundamentalist also tends to be more of a contrarian than a Firm Salesman. Whereas Firm Salesmen generally recommend popular stocks (stocks that are being recommended by others), the true Fundamentalist tends to favor stocks out of favor. In fact, if his firm or some other firm recommends his stock, he is more likely to become a seller rather than a buyer. In the opinion of the most true Fundamentalists, when a stock begins to get such recommendations, it means the stock is already fairly valued.

Lacking the true Fundamentalist's expertise, Firm Salesmen tend to be more cautious. Many hesitate to have their customers on margin. Most true Fundamentalists, in contrast, use margin freely when they think they have a solid situation, especially if the yield of the stock covers the bulk of the interest charges. The fact that the true Fundamentalist generally manages larger accounts that can afford to take bigger risks also plays a role, as does the general rule that margin accounts have assets of $25,000 or more in the market.

The more cautious approach of the Firm Salesman is reflected in other ways. Many Firm Salesmen have moved significant amounts of their clients' money into Efficient Market funds. This is most likely to occur if the salesman's firm has such a proprietary fund of its own. Others have become sellers of covered options: They recommend a specific stock purchase coupled with the sale of options on the stock. Such transactions are sold as "no risk" situations, which to a large extent they are. As has become painfully clear in the past few years, however, they also limit the upside potential since the customer is not likely to benefit if the stock goes up appreciably. This is why most true Fundamentalists are negative on such transactions. They are willing to sell covered options only in certain situations: the stock has not behaved very well, but he wants to maintain his position; or he has already had a pretty good move and he is milking it for a few more points. To buy a stock and sell an option at the same time, however, makes little sense to a true Fundamentalist. If he wants to invest for a fixed return, he is much more likely to put his customers into bonds. For similar reasons, he is also unlikely to invest in index funds.

Perhaps the most significant difference between the true Fundamentalist and the Firm Salesman is their own involvement in the market. The true Fundamentalist nearly always follows his own advice. If he's recommending a purchase strongly, he's usually also buying it for himself. Few Firm Salesmen do this. Those who do invest generally invest in companies very different from those they recommend. They tend to play with much more speculative stocks and to rely much more on tips. A sizable number of Firm Salesmen never even invest in the market, explaining that it is wrong for them to be investing their own money, since it would serve to cloud their objectivity and force them to divert too much attention to their own accounts.

There are exceptions to all of these patterns. Some Firm Salesmen invest their own money in the stocks they recommend; some recommend only a few companies. Some are more technically than fundamentally oriented. They are the exception, however, because once a broker decides to follow the recommendations of his firm he is almost committed to the other attitudes and behaviors discussed above. In this respect, the Firm Salesman is as much constrained by his view of the market as any True Believer. As we shall see, the same situation holds for the other types of salesmen.

Most Firm Salesmen are, in sociological terms, organizational men. This is not true of most True Believers. Admittedly, Ann Klein would like to become an analyst, which would in effect make her more a part of the firm. It is also true that many successful True Believers become partners. In all cases, however, their primary concern is to understand the market, and their primary passion is to invest and trade.

Firm Salesmen, in contrast, are generally more than willing to leave sales and market decision making behind to take a position in management. Many of the good ones are successful in making the transition. They are the recruits from whose ranks officer managers and senior sales personnel are drawn. From the firm's point of view, this makes eminently good sense. An office manager doesn't have to be a master of the market, he just has to keep a number of registered representatives in line. He has to know what is expected by the firm and how to insure that others conform to these expectations. The good Firm Salesman is ideally suited for this role.

It also helps if he is a good producer—has generated significant commissions. It is difficult for someone to push a specific approach with other brokers if it hasn't worked for him. As a result, it often happens that the more successful Firm Salesmen are Firm Salesmen for a relatively short period. (This has implications for the average investor, to which we shall return after we have visited with some of the other types of salesmen who frequent the market.) Before leaving the Firm Salesman, however, I want to underscore the major changes that have occurred over the last few decades, since the other sales types to be examined share many of these changes.

Nearly all Firm Salesmen have become significantly more sophisticated in recent years. They all have access to much more information than was the case just ten years ago. As such, though they tend to favor the Fundamentalist information provided to them by their firms, they also make use of both the technological information and metamarket overviews provided. Any competent salesperson today can talk about global markets, exchange rates, political implications, and the other factors impacting the market. They have access through the computers on their desks to an overwhelming amount of information, much of which comes predigested and analyzed. They similarly have access to many more products than did their counterparts of only ten years ago. They are no longer limited to selling stocks. They have a wide range of mutual funds, insurance, real estate, bonds, options, and futures, packaged in a variety of ways, available for sale. But in the end, given that nearly all of these products are provided by the salesman's firm, coupled with the fact that the firms present these products as economically attractive products, the basic character of the Firm Salesman remains remarkably stable.

MANAGING CUSTOMERS

The Firm Salesman may be the most common type of broker, but what I call the Customer Salesman best fits the common stereotype of a stockbroker. One or two can be found in nearly any brokerage office, and, they are quite visible since they tend to be outgoing and talkative. They are full of ideas and usually on the go, both literally and figuratively. They tend to be among the more successful salesmen, but they are also the most difficult brokers to pin down conceptually. The reason for this is quite simple: A Customer Salesman will tell you what you want to hear. This requires its own skill; a successful Customer Salesman must be a good social psychologist.

The Firm Salesman focuses on his product—the stocks being recommended by his firm—but the Customer Salesman focuses on his customers. He wants to know the degree of risk they're willing to take, the types of companies they like, how much capital they have to invest, the types of stories they like, and their tax situation.

In order to get this information, the Customer Salesman tries to stay in close contact with his customers. He encourages them to call him regularly, even if they're not about to make a specific trade. If he doesn't hear from them for a period of time, he will call them even if it is only to say hello. He'll also try, when possible, to initiate frequent meetings. In sum, he will attempt to make it a personal relationship rather than a strictly business one.

Such an approach does not work with all customers. They must have a fairly strong interest in the market; they must enjoy talking about it in general terms. A customer who is only interested in buying stocks that will appreciate in value is more likely to be put off by such attention than impressed by it. The customer must also have a degree of market sophistication, or at least believe he or she does, for without such sophistication, much of the broker's information will be meaningless.

This last point bears on the similarities and differences among Customer Salesmen and true Insiders. Like the Insider, the Customer Salesman is interested in information as to who is buying and who is selling. He is not interested in this information for its intrinsic value, but rather because it reflects the dynamics of the market that interest his customers. The ideal customer for a Customer Salesman is someone who wants to be part of the market, who wants to know what is going on.

A Customer Salesman aptly revealed this in describing one of his best clients. The customer was semiretired. He had built up a very successful candy business but felt that life was passing him by. He made a good living, he felt he was bright and interesting, but when he went out socially, he had nothing to talk about. The market had changed all of this for him. Because of the market, or more correctly his relationship with this particular broker, he had become a star attraction. Whatever the market news, he had something to add to the conversation.

It takes up a good deal of time to provide such services. A Firm Salesman, with his numerous small accounts, couldn't provide such service even if he wanted to. A Customer Salesman can because, for the most part, his customers' desire to be part of the market leads them to trade more. Their assets may be no greater than those of the customers of the Firm Salesman, but they generate substantially more commissions.

By focusing upon the desires and interests of his customers, the Customer Salesman provides a cushion for himself similar to that provided to the Firm Salesman who goes along with the recommendations of his firm. When things go wrong, the Customer Salesman can usually point out to his customer that it was as much his decision to buy a particular stock as it was the broker's. In fact, most Customer Salesmen lead their clients, but they do so by using their clients' preferences and biases in a manner that allows them to convince their customers that they were active participants in the decision.

The Customer Salesman's approach, however, is more dangerous. Once a firm makes a recommendation, it cannot deny it did so; they can come out with a new report hedging their original report, but the original report is still public information. Customers can, and often do, deny that they ever had any enthusiasm for a particular situation, especially if it goes sour.

There is always a risk of a customer turning in this way, but the risk is greatest when the salesman uses a customer's hunch. Most customers are more willing to admit that they had agreed with the broker (that the situation sounded good, given his information) than that their instincts were wrong. The flip side is that it is usually easier to make a sale when a customer has a hunch. A successful Customer Salesman has to walk this narrow line. In any given situation, his decision is influenced by what he knows of the customer. He approaches more warily those customers with a history of "turning" than those who take reverses in stride.

To minimize the risk of customers turning, many Customer Salesmen attempt to convince their customers that customers are sophisticated investors. Even when rejecting a customer's suggestion, a Customer Salesman is supportive and likely to point out the merits of the suggestion. Such treatment serves not only to keep the customers happy but also to provide a foundation for the sharing of responsibility.

What are Customer Salesmen's true feelings about their customers? Like most market professionals, they have a fairly low opinion of lay investors. Their reasons for belittling lay investors, however, differ from those of the Firm Salesmen, who criticize their customers' lack of understanding and laziness. Customer Salesmen emphasize the customers' arrogance and greed. Every Customer Salesman has a story about having a customer who pushed him into doing one thing, only to have the customer turn around and blame the Salesman later. There seem to be an equal number of stories about customers who had to be pushed into a situation and who then took the credit for themselves when the stock did well. To a large extent, Customer Salesmen create these problems, since they feed into their customers' images of themselves as astute investors. Most brokers know this and admit it; but they still get very upset when they have to deal with such situations.

Customer Salesmen do, however, have a slightly higher opinion of at least some of their own customers. Many have a number of relatively sophisticated, more experienced accounts. This is understandable since it is primarily only experienced investors who are comfortable with the Customer Salesman. Even the most arrogant person has some idea of his or her limitations, and it takes some knowledge of the market to follow a Customer Salesman.

A Customer Salesman needs to believe that some of his customers know what he is doing, since he requires sources of information and his customers constitute an important source of such information. Most salesmen rely primarily upon professional sources, but the more sources the better. Nearly every Customer Salesman I have met has one or two accounts whose opinions he respects. Such customers are usually other market professionals, exbrokers, or persons with good business connections. Another factor which leads Customer Salesmen to value their own customers more highly than other customers is the fact that Customer Salesmen are very personable as a rule and simply come to like their own customers.

Most Customer Salesmen have little or no respect for their own firm's research; many comment that it's junk, especially those who work for the smaller Wall Street firms. Lack of what they believe to be good research doesn't bother them, however, since they don't rely on research. They do value highly, though, the reputation of the firm itself. This makes sense, because a firm with a good reputation, which is financially sound and which has a good back office, gives customers a sense of confidence, which goes toward maintaining good customer relations.

That being said, Customer Salesmen are likely to praise the research of other firms, regardless of the firm for which they work. This may seem to be a simple case of some firms having better research than others, but it is not. Think about it: The Customer Salesman is in the business of relaying information. Reports put out by his own firm don't qualify as information; they are firm recommendations. Reports that he is able to acquire from other firms, however, do constitute information, and it is information a customer can get only through his broker. As a result, another firm's reports serve to strengthen the tie between broker and customer, whereas recommendations from one's own firm put the firm between the broker and customer.

A successful Customer Salesman is often approached by other firms. For most firms, such "headhunting" is good business. It is not just that such brokers generate a lot of business and hence firm income, but also that they are in a position to bring most of their clientele with them. This generally is not the case with even the most successful Firm Salesmen. The Firm Salesman's customers have been buying the firm's product, not the salesman's product.

Though most successful Customer Salesmen are temperamentally not organizational men, many do accept management positions. In nearly all cases, however, they insist upon maintaining their own accounts. The successful Firm Salesman who moves into management often cuts back on his own accounts to focus attention upon organizational problems, but the Firm Salesman who moves into management is likely to serve as a model for other brokers. Rather than checking up on his fellow brokers, he is expected to help them improve their sales techniques. In some cases, even this is not expected; he is rather given a management position and the added income that comes with such a position simply to keep him within the firm.

In light of the great similarities between Customer Salesmen and true Insiders, one might ask what the differences are. It is a question of priorities and basic goals. The true Insider is interested in collecting information in order to understand what is happening, with the goal of mastering the market. The Customer Salesman is interested in selling stocks. The true Insider is not interested in just any story or any piece of information; he's very selective. He is not likely to give much weight to what his customers have to say, nor is he interested in information bearing on institutional activities if he feels such information has already been discounted. The Customer Salesman will make use of any and all information that he feels could affect a sale. He is as likely to make use of economic information (earnings projections) and technical information (chartist reports) as information dealing with who is buying and who is selling.

The true Insider tries to restrict himself to "firsthand" information, but the Customer Salesman is perfectly happy to use secondary and even tertiary information. This is not to imply that good Customer Salesmen will use any information they get their hands on. They know that you can have too much of a good thing; they also know that putting their customers into too many bad situations will destroy business in the long run. The most important thing, however, for most Customer Salesmen is that the information "sounds good."

Earlier it was noted that Firm Salesmen require reports on more companies than do true Fundamentalists. The same can be said for Customer Salesmen vis-à-vis true Insiders. The true Insider, like the true Fundamentalist, is content to find those few situations that he feels will work out. A Customer Salesman can't survive with a few situations. His customers differ, and he must have situations for all of them. This is why he must rely on secondary and tertiary sources of information. He cannot afford to put in the time that a true Insider does following up on a single story. A true Insider like Hank Strong will visit different houses and talk to various people; the Customer Salesman must rely on information that he can glean during and between telephone calls with his clients.

The biggest difference, however, is the one that was mentioned earlier in our discussion of Firm Salesmen. Customer Salesmen, like Firm Salesmen, are not heavily involved in the market for basically the same reasons. They feel that if they were deeply involved in the market, they could not be as objective or give their accounts the attention they require. Customer Salesmen differ from Firm Salesmen in that most have a history of personal involvement, though few have been successful. Many, if not most, Customer Salesmen, in fact, became brokers by virtue of the personal contacts they established while customers themselves. Many even hoped to make their fortunes through their own investments. As they saw their commission incomes dissipate in the market, they concluded that their energies were better spent in attempting to develop a clientele rather than in trying to beat the market.

There is one way in which Customer Salesmen are similar to true Insiders. Like Insiders, they take a negative view toward government regulations. They are willing to admit that such regulations protect customers from unscrupulous brokers and firms, but most add that in the end governmental interference with the free market actually hurts their clients more than it helps them. When pushed as to what should be done to protect the small investor, nearly all respond that brokers must be made to deal more honestly with their customers. With many, "honesty" seems to be an obsession. In part, no doubt, this is due to their own misgivings about the way that they treat their customers. It can also be seen as highlighting once more the Customer Salesmen's all-important customer-broker relationship.

In most respects, Customer Salesmen have probably changed less than most other types of brokers during the last twenty years. Like most everyone else, they have been affected by the growth and spread of both information and products. This growth and the rapid dissemination of information have created difficulties for the true Insider but have simply provided more material for the talented Customer Salesman to use in constructing his own accounts. The proliferation of products has also been more of an asset than a deficit. There are simply more products available to match to the particular needs and interests of different customers. The technological growth of Wall Street itself has proven to be another benefit. Since a Customer Salesman is less dependent upon his firm than the Firm Salesperson, more and more successful Customer Salesmen operate as quasi-independent brokers, thanks to computers and telecommunication technology. Rather than commuting to an office of a major firm and functioning as an employee of such a firm, they have been able to set up their own offices and enter into a contract relationship with a member firm to provide it with the back-office and trading support required. Although the major attraction of such an arrangement is the promise of being able to retain a larger percentage of income generated, a secondary, but very important attraction is that it further solidifies the customer-broker tie.

11

SELLING THE MARKET

As Firm Salesmen mirror Fundamentalists and Customer Salesmen mirror Insiders, what I have chosen to call Market Salesmen reflect the Cyclist-Chartists and the Efficient Market adherents seeing the market as governed by its own rhythms and patterns.[45] The salesmen differ in that they are not concerned with mastering or explaining this "order," whichever one it may be. What they share with both the Cyclist-Chartist and the Efficient Market adherent is a view of the market as basically an autonomous entity. They may or may not have specific views as to whether people ought to be buying or selling parts or all of this market, but Market Salesmen accept the fact that their own livelihood is dependent upon people doing just that. In short, they see themselves as order takers who are willing, able, and required to provide a range of information and services to facilitate such transactions.

Market Salesmen must be ready to comment on many more stocks than an Ann Klein, who limits her customers to those stocks that she personally follows. Market Salesmen are first and foremost salesmen and as such must be able to comment on the stocks that are of interest to their customers. As a result, they cannot rely on their own charts; they simply do not have the time, nor in most cases the ability, to maintain the number of charts that would be required. They are forced, consequently, to depend upon the charts and services of others, primarily those of advisory services—or, if available, those of their firm. Most Market Salesmen are more than willing to do this; it is easier, and the charts and recommendations of their firm or of a known advisory service generally carry more weight with their customers than would their own.

There are nonideological reasons in the making of most Market Salesmen. Quite simply, many brokers who adopt the Market Salesman style cannot function as Firm Salesmen or Customer Salesmen. In some cases, they work for firms which do not supply them with a sufficient number of in-house recommendations. Others are just uncomfortable with the Firm Salesman approach. Few have the temperament to function as Customer Salesmen or the ability to establish the contacts or the clientele that this approach requires.

While few Market Salesmen are such by choice, they would appear on the surface to be ideal brokers. In fact, their actions are most in keeping with the official job description of a broker put out by the New York Stock Exchange: to execute customer orders and to provide the backup services and advice that customers may request. Nevertheless, Market Salesmen (or order takers, which is what most really are) have historically often seemed to be ducks out of water, much as have their True Believer counterparts, the Cyclist-Chartists and the Efficient Market adherents.

In contrast to most Firm Salesmen and Customer Salesmen, Market Salesmen often lack a well-formulated sales pitch. They often seem unable to get a firm handle on the market; many even appear to be overwhelmed by it. Their problem is not that they are more ignorant of the ways of the market than other salesmen; their problem is that they tend to be much more eclectic and consequently less focused. When they feel that they are in tune with the market, usually as a result of one of their advisory services being correct for a change, they can become very aggressive salesmen. At these times, they function very much like an Ann Klein except that they use the recommendations of others. When they feel that they are not in tune with the market, however— usually as a result of their pet advisory service being wrong—they tend to become very passive. During these periods, they are likely to function merely as order takers.

Market Salesmen are often among the more critical denizens of Wall Street. They tend to be critical of their firm, of other firms, of other salesmen, and of most customers. In this respect, they are much like their True Believer counterparts, the Cyclist-Chartist and Efficient Market adherents. Unlike the Cyclist-Chartist and Efficient Market adherents, they generally try to camouflage their true feelings, though some don't do a very good job of it. They realize that they must maintain an upbeat presentation of self if they are to generate any business. Many manage to maintain this posture by hoping that tomorrow they will be able to latch onto the "right" service. Few expect to find an advisory service that will provide them with sure market winners; rather they hope for a service in which they can believe and that will enable them to generate sufficient business to earn a comfortable living. At other times, they contemplate moving their customers into index funds, but then they wonder how they will make a living.

Unlike the true Cyclist-Chartist and Efficient Market adherents, most Market Salesmen have historically been prone to fairly low self-esteem. In part this has been due to the ribbing and criticism they have received from their co-workers and management because (1) they were generally only marginal producers, (2) they tended not to be good team players, and (3) as a group they lacked the sociability characteristic of Customer Salesmen. In addition, most have felt that their relative lack of success was due, in some measure, to their own inability to get a proper handle on the market. It was a status, in short, that most everyone hoped would be transitional—a younger salesman, especially in a firm with limited in-house research, for example, trying to get established; or an older salesman who had tried some other approach, failed, and was trying to find his way. There were few, if any, places in management for them; most firms, in fact, preferred not to have them around at all. As a result, a Market Salesman's career was likely to consist of moving from firm to firm, with each new firm being slightly less prestigious than the one left. Many eventually found themselves out of the brokerage world.

Time, however, seems to have helped the Market Salesman in two fundamental ways: (1) discount houses, and (2) the growth of mutual funds, especially index funds. To put the matter quite simply, the same traits that once worked against Market Salesmen now work in their favor. It was noted above, for example, that Market Salesmen tend to function almost exclusively as order takers when things are not going well. This type of passive orientation used to receive little if any managerial encouragement, but things have changed with the growth of discount houses. A Market Salesman willing to function as an efficient, trained order taker has acquired value and is ideally suited for such a position. In most discount operations, the Market Salesman deals with more sophisticated investors and is not expected to make specific recommendations; his interest in the market as a whole and technical orientation makes him of great value, however, to such sophisticated investors. Much the same can be said for the Market Salesman's proclivity toward index funds. Where previously putting funds into an index fund was seen to be a form of surrender, today it is seen as downright smart. Admittedly, such an approach cannot generate the revenues per customer of a successful Firm Salesman or Customer Salesman. The growth in discount houses and mutual funds, however, provides a depth of customers that makes it possible to do very well. How well is unclear, but most Market Salesmen are better off today than they were twenty years ago.

Though it is always difficult to make predictions when it comes to the market, I would hazard a guess that Market Salesmen will continue to prosper in the coming years. My expectation is based on the continuing growth of investments in mutual funds, Keogh plans, regular IRAs, and Roth IRAs. If a decision is ever made to transfer a percentage of social security payments into the stock market, the demand for Market Salesmen is likely to increase even more.

12

SELLING THE ACTION AND DREAMS

Few people on Wall Street stimulate as great an emotional response as Action Salesmen. They are loved and hated, often by the same people, and sometimes at the same time. Why? Because the Action Salesman supplies his customers with "action." He is not there to offer safe investments; most Action Salesmen are not even concerned with making you money. Rather, they're there to allow you to participate in the excitement and drama of the market; they are there to give you some "kicks" and to help you vent whatever gambling instincts you might have.

It may seem as if investors hardly need anyone to help them do this, and that therefore it requires little or no skill to be an Action Salesman. Nothing could be farther from the truth; it requires more skill to be a successful Action Salesman than any other type of salesman. The market is not all action; for every exciting situation there are a score of dull investments. The Action Salesman must know where the action is and where it is likely to be in the future. Furthermore, he must be able to move his customers in and out of situations with as little damage as possible. All of this requires a sophisticated feel for the market.

The concept of "feel" is central to understanding the Action Salesmen. It is also this feel for the market that relates the Action Salesman to his major true believer counterpart, the Trader. Like Traders, Action Salesmen have an emotional relationship to the market. In this respect, they are similar to Customer Salesmen, but whereas Customer Salesmen are primarily concerned with the psychological needs of their customers, Action Salesmen are tuned into the social-psychological mood of the market itself. And like the True Believer Transformational Idea adherent, they can recognize and spin a good story.

Action Salesmen, like Traders, see the market as a game. Like Traders, they are usually addicted to the tape. Unlike Traders, they're not committed to winning. The Trader attempts to separate himself from his emotions and to use his emotions as a guide—which more often than not means going against his emotions—but the Action Salesman rides the emotional tides of the market. Unlike the Trader, who attempts to master the market, the Action Salesman is primarily interested in sales. To the Action Salesman, the emotional moods of the market are not tools for understanding why the market behaves as it does, but rather tools for obtaining market orders. He is not there to get his customers to control their emotions, but rather to enable them to experience emotional exhilaration.

Most Action Salesmen project an image similar to that of the Customer Salesmen—outgoing and gregarious; if anything, they tend to be more "flashy." They are, however, more interested in the market than their customers. Customer Salesmen are always trying to enhance their customers; Action Salesmen are always trying to enhance the market. It is the market that they like to talk about and dream about. In this respect, they are like Sarah Wright, and even Ann Klein and John Holland, though their main concern is: "Can I sell it?"

Action Salesmen are very aggressive. Timing is all important. If one wants to catch an explosive situation, one must be willing to move quickly. If one waits even a day or two, the excitement may be all over. Consequently, Action Salesmen pressure their customers to move at once when they think the time is right. A real Fundamentalist is likely to purchase a stock in response to an unexpected spurt in earning, and a real Trader may respond to price momentum, but the Action Salesman attempts to use the excitement of something happening to make a trade. He often doesn't care that much whether it is a buy or sell order as long as there is an order.

To be successful, however, an Action Salesman must be aware of the likes and dislikes, fears and hopes, of his customers. Most of his customers like action or they wouldn't trade through him. However, some like and can take more action than others. A good Action Salesman must know what different customers can handle, both emotionally and financially. If he tries to push a conservative customer too hard, he can lose him entirely; he is just as likely to lose a "high roller" by not providing him with enough action.

Action Salesmen make use of different types of investments. Most focus upon the heavily traded glamour stocks, which are more prone to give customers a ride for their money. Their propensity to trade in volume makes them highly visible stocks, and these are also the types of stocks about which there are also most likely to be stories. Even when they are not moving one way or another, the Action Salesman's customers are likely to feel that they are still in the middle of things. They can follow these stocks more easily since they are normally mentioned in the market reports carried by many radio stations.[46]

The heavily traded glamour stocks have another advantage: They are easier to get in and out of. This is important to the Action Salesman, because though he is not primarily concerned with making money for his customers, neither does he want them to be wiped out. He must be able to get his customers out quickly if things start to go wrong. Again, this is similar to John Holland's approach, though John Holland is likely to get out only when he doesn't like the way the stock is acting; the Action Salesman might have to get out because his customer cannot take it any more.

Though Action Salesmen like heavily traded glamour stocks, many also have an affection for their opposite—thinly traded secondary stocks. Here they are willing to give up some of the safety of heavy action for what may be potentially even greater volatility. The situation is analogous to a preference for playing red and black at roulette or for playing specific numbers. Many Action Salesmen play both types of stocks, depending upon the preferences of their customers; other stick with one type or another.

Most Action Salesmen have traded their own accounts in the past, and most claim that they still like to trade for themselves. In fact, it is almost impossible for anyone to function as an Action Salesman who has not traded for himself; there is just no other way to develop a feel for the market. Most will freely admit, however, that they seldom do very well for themselves. Many even wish that they could refrain from trading completely; they often add that they would be a lot richer if they could stop. In short, Action Salesmen, like Firm Salesmen and Customer Salesmen, realize that the only way they are going to make any money is through the business they can generate. At one time in their lives, they may have had hopes of becoming successful Traders like John Holland; now, most realize that the most they can hope for is to be a successful salesman. Few imagine themselves ever becoming converts to Sarah Wright's view of the market. To them, a story is a selling tool, not a picture of the future.

Though some Action Salesmen have adjusted to this situation gracefully, most are tinged with some bitterness. This bitterness influences their view of the market and their opinions of those involved in the market. A few are willing to admit that there are some successful Traders, but most claim that there is no such thing. The Trader who makes it big one year, in their opinion, will ninety-nine times out of a hundred lose it all the next year. Their attitudes toward Fundamentalists, Insiders, and Cyclist-Chartists are basically the same. As far as most Action Salesmen are concerned, anyone who thinks that he can beat the market is just kidding himself.

This cynicism colors their view of management, money managers, and lay investors, though it takes a slightly different form in each case. They are most negative on management, because they believe that management knows the market cannot be beaten; they similarly have contempt for money managers who think they can beat the market. It is only the lay investor for whom they have any sympathy, because "he doesn't know any better."

Given this attitude, one might wonder why most Action Salesmen don't just quit. It's because beating the market is not what it is all about. They are in the market because it is exciting, and they believe that is why most investors are in the market. To put their customers into mutual funds or other more "stable" investments wouldn't make their customers rich, and it would take away the one thing that the market has to offer—namely, excitement. Action Salesmen are not willing to deprive their customers of this; furthermore, they don't think that is what their customers would want them to do even if they knew the market can't be beaten.

Action Salesmen acquire a different type of clientele than the clientele of other types of salesmen. In part, this is by customer choice. Many customers have had a number of past brokers with whom they were unsatisfied. Only when they found an Action Salesman did they feel that they were getting their money's worth. In part, it is due to the Action Salesmen, most of whom are very wary of dealing with customers who are not willing, in fact eager, to trade. They are uncomfortable with the accounts of "widows and orphans." If such accounts come their way, they are more than likely to direct them elsewhere, if they insist on staying, to put them into nonvolatile situations and forget about them.

Given their negative view of other market professionals, one might expect that Action Salesmen would be subject to some of the same abuse historically allotted to Market Salesmen. This is seldom the case because there is one major difference between them: even the average Action Salesman tends to be a good producer. First, most of his clients are fairly wealthy; second, he trades them a great deal. Whatever management might think of him, they are not about to send him on his way.

For his part, the Action Salesman is not about to go anywhere either. First of all, there is really no place for him in institutional sales. Institutions (pension funds, banks, mutual funds, and the like) are not in the market to play games; even if they wanted to, they couldn't. Government regulations, plus the institutional process of decision making, make it impossible for such institutions to trade the market the way an Action Salesman does. There is similarly no place for him in management. True, as with a successful Customer Salesman, a very successful Action Salesman may be made a partner to keep him, but he will not have any management role. Most firms already have enough managers who are market cynics. Finally, and most important, even if such a position were offered him, the average Action Salesman wouldn't take it, because to do so would mean cutting back on his own trading and removing him from the action that he loves. Many wish they could do it, but most admit that they are addicted to the daily action.

One might legitimately ask whether the Action Salesman is a dying breed. He clearly seems to be fighting the trend. Moreover, the speed with which information is not only dissipated but also analyzed makes his job more difficult. The key issue for survival, however, hinges on success. The poor and modest producers are probably a dying breed; management doesn't like the image they give Wall Street. The successful ones, however, will be around as long as there is a market, because there are people who are more interested in the excitement of the market than in making money. As long as such people exist and as long as the market can satisfy their needs, the Action Salesman will remain a part of the market.

With the Action Salesman, we complete our analysis of the basic types of salesmen, each a counterpart to one or more True Believer. Whereas our True Believers are convinced that their versions enable them to master the market, we have seen how salespersons are adept at using such versions to sell stocks. We have not yet, however, examined all of the ways these versions are used. One more way is simply to "explain" or, more exactly, rationalize the market in hindsight. Put slightly differently, they are used to resolve uncertainties and ambiguities by showing that what occurred was understandable, and perhaps even unavoidable, if framed properly.

All "explanations" seek to explain, but their tones differ considerably. In some cases, there tends to be a detached tone to the explanation; in other cases, a more upbeat spin; and in yet others a decidedly bitter, negative tone. Historically the detached voice has been the most common, with the upbeat and cynical voices about equal. The unprecedented rise in the market since the late eighties has clearly changed this distribution. We still have our undecided, our bears, and our bulls, but the dominant voices have been those of the bulls. The emergence of the Efficient Market theory—which is itself really a neutral explanation as to why you can't outperform the market—as an investment strategy underscores this fact quite dramatically. You don't need to pick stocks anymore; all you have to do is invest. This is clearly a very optimistic viewpoint.

There are others, however, who hold a much more cynical position. In my earlier book on the market I contrasted such a cynic with Dave Gibbons, who at that time I treated as a more neutral rationalizer. Such cynics have not had much of an audience of late, but I believe they represent a view that deserves to be heard if for no other reason than it helps us better grasp the full richness of the mind of the market. Once we have heard from such a cynic, we will be in a better position to appreciate those with more faith.

PART IV

CYNICISM, FAITH, AND FOOLISHNESS

13

A MARKET CYNIC

For Market Cynics, the market has a sinister character, which they are more than willing to publicize. This makes them an embarrassment to the market, and most market professionals wish that they would disappear. To a large extent, this wish has been fulfilled in recent years, as the great bull market has driven most of these cynics to the sidelines. Nevertheless, cynics have historically constituted a fairly large group and will surely return in greater numbers when this bull market ends. Consequently, they still deserve our attention.

True Believers seek to understand and "beat" the market; salesmen try to sell stocks. The cynics want to explain why things went wrong. But what explanations do they give? Ironically, though not surprisingly, explanations are framed in terms of the same overviews of the market used by True Believers and salesmen.

One may ask why any broker would become a cynic. The answer is quite simple: Most are unable to function as either a successful True Believer or as a salesman. They have tried and failed, and are now primarily concerned with explaining this failure. How do they do this?

Those with a Fundamentalist bias tend to stress the irrationality of the market—their "undervalued" stocks have not gone up because the market is crazy. Those with an Insider bias complain about their lack of information and the conspiratorial nature of the market. Those with a Cyclist-Chartist bias bemoan the deceptions and traps inherent in market cycles. Those with a Trader bias curse their bad luck. Those who favor the Efficient Market rhetoric tend also to fault their luck, and those with an inclination for the grand story are prone to note how dreams can turn into nightmares. Most cynics, however, make use

of whatever "explanation" seems appropriate at the time. Salesmen may be
more eclectic than True Believers, but cynics are the most eclectic of all.

Despite their admitted failures, cynics can have a real influence on the market. In fact, they are often the clearest spokespersons for the various market
philosophies, though seldom in an integrated way. Investors who have lost
money are generally more interested in knowing why they lost than those who
have made money are in knowing why they made money. Losers want an explanation, preferably one that doesn't make them look foolish. The cynics are able
to provide such explanations. The various market philosophies discussed above
are implicit in what the True Believers and salesmen do, but they are explicitly
presented by the cynics.

In order to have a better understanding of such cynics, I think that, as with
the True Believers and salespersons, it makes sense to get to know one of
them more intimately; in many ways, when you know one, you know them all.
Unfortunately, the great bull market of the last decade has thinned their ranks,
or at least made them more difficult to locate. I have elected therefore to move
back in time and to revisit the same cynic spokesperson I introduced in my
earlier book, Henry Geller. Henry Geller, I should add, has a decided bias for
the Insider view of the market; he could be called a Tipster. I originally selected his particular type because it is the most common; he also best reflects
the essential quality of cynics. As in the case of the True Believers, I have
camouflaged some of his personal characteristics. The time is approximately
1980.

Henry Geller had been in the market nearly as long as Bill Chester had: about
forty years. His father, with whom he never got on too well, was a successful
broker but lost much of the family's money during the 1929 crash. From the
time he was young, Henry always wanted to be a broker. The family name and
portfolio were still good enough in the early forties to land him a job with a
small but respected house. Since then, Henry Geller had worked for four different firms; these relocations had not always occurred under the most amica-
ble of conditions. At the time I met him, Mr. Geller was with one of the larger
retail firms. He was not among their best producers, though he made a reasonable living. This was reflected in his "office worker" appearance.

Henry Geller described himself as "basically a Fundamentalist." In addition,
he claimed to keep his own charts and to follow a number of the chart services.
He was, however, neither a true Fundamentalist nor a true Cyclist-Chartist; he
was, if anything, a "Tipster." In his own words, "It is not what you know in this

business, it is who you know." As far as Henry Geller was concerned, his problem was that he didn't know the right people. This attitude was reflected in
almost everything Henry Geller had to say regarding the market.

Henry Geller's firm put out numerous reports. Whereas most of his cowork-
ers relied heavily on these reports, Henry Geller felt that they were useless.
"By the time I get a chance to see one of these reports, all the big guys have
already seen it and acted on it." He had no interest in these reports as sources
of information; he was only interested in the final recommendation, to buy or
sell. He felt this way about all such reports. He didn't care if the house putting
out the recommendation was a big house or a small house, a firm with market
muscle or one with no reputation at all.

This concern for buying and selling was reflected in Henry Geller's stance
on charts. Charts are useful, he claims, because they tell you if the stock is
being bought or sold. He was consequently more interested in chart movements than in chart patterns; in this respect he differed from most Cyclist-
Chartists. As he said, "When you see a lot of buying going on in a stock, you
know that someone knows something. You can't really know what is going on
unless you are one of the big boys on the inside, but the charts can help you."
This attitude toward those who know and those who don't, including himself,
pervaded his whole outlook on the market. "Those guys upstairs never tell us
anything unless it is too late to do anything."

Henry Geller's "take" on those who are and those who are not in the know
determined not only how he saw the market but also how he saw his customers,
what he read, to whom he talked. On the whole, Henry Geller had a very
negative view of customers; as far as he was concerned, less than 10 percent
knew what they were doing—and those only because of their own contacts. "It
doesn't matter how successful they are, but who they know." One of his best
customers, Henry Geller told me, was a guy who didn't trade much, but his
brother was a president of a big bank and he got all sorts of good information.
"My barber is also a good contact, because he hears all sorts of things from his
customers, who include some of the biggest guys on the street."

It is consistent with Henry Geller's view regarding inside information that
he didn't see, or even look for, general market trends. "You have to stick with
the companies with the story regardless of what the market is doing." When
asked how he could separate the good story from the bad story, he answered,
"It's the guys with money who know what's going on." Here he added, "You
have to be very careful, because when you make money, your customer will
take the credit, but if he loses any money, it is your [the broker's] fault." On

this point, most brokers agree, but few seem to feel the injustice of it all as strongly as Henry Geller did.

Though Henry Geller saw the road to riches paved with good information, by which he meant private information, he saw his own survival as being based upon his ability to generate confidence among his own customers. This he tried to do by maintaining personal contact, especially with his larger accounts. As far as he was concerned, mail was useless except for bringing in a few new accounts. "People don't want to read about a company; they want to know if they can make some money. The phone is okay, but really you have to go out and see them."

Henry Geller saw most of his customers as not only ignorant but also greedy. He condemned this greed but claimed he had adjusted to it. "I'd prefer to buy blue-chip companies, but with my customers I have to buy smaller companies. My customers like them because you can get better moves out of them since their stocks trade in less volume. Smaller companies respond better to stories and rumors than do large companies."

Similarly, although asserting the virtues of holding stocks for long-term gains, he claimed that most of his customers wanted to take their profits. He admitted that he often supported this approach because it generated more business—"Why should I fight them; it's their money"—and added, "There is also constant pressure from upstairs to move stocks. You've go to do some business every day around here if you want to be kept."

Henry Geller dismissed the normal sources of information—"By the time the information is public, it is of little use"—and, in much the same way, although he talked about good buying and bad buying, he didn't follow most of the more popular indicators of such buying. He was unfamiliar, for example, with the "odd-lot" figures, which in the 1980s were a widely used sentiment indicator that functioned much like put/call ratios do today. His answer, when questioned about the use of the odd-lot figures, was quite characteristic of him. "That's good information, but I can't get a hold of them." (They were published daily in both the *New York Times* and the *Wall Street Journal,* two papers he claimed to read everyday.) In all of these respects, he differed from Hank Strong who, in addition to relying on his "inside" information, made extensive use of public sources.

Though Henry Geller's market philosophies served primarily to justify his own lack of success, it would be misleading to interpret his view of the market purely as an example of "sour grapes." It was also due as much to his sense of "the world against Henry Geller." Even on those rare occasions when he was riding high, he saw the world as out to get him.

Henry Geller did not care what the value of a company was, providing someone with substantial financial resources was willing to buy it. Similarly, he didn't want to hold on to a company no matter how underpriced if someone with a large position in the stock was selling. This does not mean that Henry Geller felt that economic factors were irrelevant; remember that he claimed to be a Fundamentalist, of sorts. What it does mean is that he felt that most published economic information was of questionable veracity. He was fond of pointing out how a company can juggle its books to either hide or increase earnings. In short, the economic facts are not facts until people in the know have verified them. "The way these people verify such facts is by buying and selling. The earnings picture on a company might be bad, but if a big mutual fund is buying, then they must know something." Similarly, the future for another company might look good, but if the president is selling, he did not want to wait until the bad news became public.

When questioned about the soundness of this approach, given the relatively bad record—at that time—of mutual funds, insiders, and trust departments, Mr. Geller merely smiled. Again, it was clearly a question of not believing the public information. "I don't believe any of that stuff. That's why I'm a contrarian" (a person who prefers to go against the dominant market trend). "The big boys often use market moods for their own advantage. When they are trying to buy, they like to put out pessimistic predictions, and when they are trying to sell, they like to put out optimistic predictions." Having watched Henry Geller over a period of time, however, I would say that he went with the tide more than against it.

To the Henry Gellers of the world, the market is a battle; one's opponents are the other investors. One's resources determine one's success. Ideally, the best resource is money. To quote: "Someone with enough money can make the market do what he wants." For the little guy with little money, it is necessary to know what the guys with the money are doing. This requires both guile and caution. Caution requires that one never expose oneself to the manipulative powers of the big boys. In line with this reasoning, Henry Geller avoided short selling and margin. "Half the time they let you short a stock, they are only setting you up to run the stock on you. They suck you in on margin, then they drop the stock on you."

Given Henry Geller's negativity toward the stock market, one might wonder why he remained a broker. He had no choice; at least he didn't feel he had—the market was all he had ever known. In addition, the combat aspect of the market fascinated him; he loved the fight, though his own nose often got bloodied. Deep down, he felt that with a few breaks he could be a winner. All that he needed was a few new customers with good contacts or a few good stories. "That is all you need, because once you get a hold of some good information, you can start trading it with the other guys. Then you are made."

If Henry Geller appears to be a fairly sad character, it is because he is. In part, this is due to his lack of success; in greater part, it is due to his cynical, almost "paranoid" view of the market and life in general. Most people in the market have one or two stories about "inside" information, but few see the market as controlled and governed by such information. Given Henry Geller's market record, his options were either to feel paranoid or to change his view of the market.

Henry Geller received a good deal of flack from his fellow brokers for always talking about the way the big boys were taking advantage of the little investor. In general, such an opinion doesn't help to generate business for most retail brokers. It certainly didn't help Henry Geller, since he put off as many customers with this line as he seduced with his own so-called inside information. Why then did he do it? Because Henry Geller was convinced that the market is one giant conspiracy. Moreover, this vision of the market was more important to him than selling stocks.

One might expect that Henry Geller and those like him would have little effect upon the way other people perceive the market. They are not held in much esteem by their fellow brokers or by their firm's managers. They have in the past, however, been spokespersons for a number of small investors. Moreover, there are times when they influence the thinking of other professionals— generally when these other professionals have experienced a particularly serious unexpected reverse. At such times, Henry Geller's view of the market can be quite consoling. The dramatic rise in the market during the last decade has lessened the numbers needing such consolation. If and when the market turns down, however, I expect the Henry Gellers of the market to find a whole new audience.

It may initially seem strange that the views of a person who is a notorious failure should ever prove to be consoling, but upon analysis it is anything but strange. Henry Geller–type views always provide an answer, if admittedly after the fact. They don't even try to provide an answer before the fact—or, more accurately, they have a built-in escape clause, namely that the market is "rigged." In short, the Henry Gellers of the market don't really care what the market is going to do but are only interested in coming to terms with what has already been done. That is why they can be consoling, and also why they are doomed to failure.

There is a very real sense, of course, that most everyone we have met so far believes that the market is rigged, if what one means by rigged is that it is highly ordered. They differ from Henry Geller insofar that they don't believe it is rigged against them. They differ among themselves—True Believers versus salespersons—to the degree to which they believe that they can discern this order ahead of time and use this knowledge. It was Henry Geller's belief that he would always be a loser, however, that most sets him apart from the others we have met. Nearly all, if not all, True Believers and salespersons accept the fact that they will be right some times and wrong at other times. All they want is to be right more than they are wrong. It was, in short, Henry Geller's fatalism that was his most defining characteristic rather than his negativism. There is something quite ironic about this. At the same time that the great bull market of the nineties has driven most of the Henry Gellers to ground, it has also served to increase the overall fatalism of the market, albeit in a positive rather than a negative way. If Henry felt that you could never win, there are plenty of new players who believe that you can never lose.

(14)

FAITH: FOLLOW THE MONEY

As irrationally cynical and negative as Henry Geller may appear, the bull market of the last decade has produced scores of equally irrational optimists. As the Henry Gellers use the rhetoric of the various True Believers to explain and justify their negativism, these optimists use whatever rhetoric they can find to justify their blind faith in the market. There is, however, one particular story line that is commonly found in these optimistic renditions. In brief, it goes like this:

> The market goes up when money comes in, and down when money goes out.
> There is a lot of money out there with no place to go but the market.
> Ergo, the market has no place to go but up.

Whether this is true or not is, of course, open to debate, and is an issue far beyond the scope of this book.[47] Fortunately, for the purposes at hand it really isn't that important whether all or any of these statements are true. It is sufficient that many people accept them as true. Why they should think so is the question that is pertinent to our concerns. What we discover, not surprisingly, is that different experts have different answers to this question that are influenced by the general market philosophies discussed earlier. More concretely, six to ten factors are normally used to flesh out this story, with the particular items varying depending upon who is telling the story. Perhaps more interesting in the context of this book is the fact that each of these different factors is given its own particular spin depending upon who is telling the story.

So what are these factors? In alphabetical order, I would note seven:

(1) alternative investments, or the lack of competitive alternative investment opportunities; (2) America, or more specifically, the privileged status of the United States as an investment haven; (3) the class structure, or more accurately the increasingly skewed distribution of capital resources that generates surplus capital for investment; (4) changing corporate structure that has led to increased capital formation; (5) demographic changes that have generated an aging population more dependent upon personal capital for economic survival; (6) the growth of pension funds of varying sorts, including a dramatic increase in Keogh plans, IRAs, and the like; and (7) technology. In one form or other, these factors are cited by optimists on Wall Street as explaining why we should expect a continuing flow of capital into the American stock market that will serve to drive the market higher and higher.

How do the different True Believers we met earlier weave these factors into their accounts? For most Fundamentalists, items 2, 4, 5, and 6 have the most legitimacy. Of these four, however, number 4 is clearly the most important. The true Fundamentalist not only believes that market value is determined by economic factors, but also that such economic factors are themselves governed by corporate efficiencies. As a group, they are similarly firm believers in the capitalist system and the advantages of rational corporate organization. Whether most corporations are in fact more rational today than they have been in the past is a question I would not attempt to answer. But it would appear as if many, maybe even all, Fundamentalists believe that this is so. This, coupled with what they see to be a more probusiness governmental stance (reflected in item 2), are what they believe has given the United States its present privileged investment status. Most are similarly favorably impressed by the growth of funds pouring into pension funds (item 6) and the demographics (item 5) that indicate that this is a trend which is likely to continue.

It is important to note, however, that most Fundamentalists have significant concerns. Others may argue that there is no real alternative to the stock market (item 1), but for true Fundamentalists there are always other alternatives to the stock market—be they bonds, real estate, cash, or even foreign markets. Admittedly, low interest rates on bonds can make stocks more attractive, but as bond rates go lower, the value of bonds with fixed rates increases, making such bonds very attractive alternative investments, especially when their comparatively low risk is factored in. Many Fundamentalists also see a downside to broadening market participation, which many other market professionals only see as a plus. What concerns these Fundamentalists is that, though broad participation provides an extra kick to the market when everything is going up, any sort of significant weakness might well become exacerbated if the public begins to panic and withdraws its money precipitously. These Fundamentalists often express a similar reservation regarding the general fascination for technology stocks. The fact that much of this money is presently invested in various index funds makes them even more nervous, since they fear that substantial withdrawal of funds will cause forced-selling in a limited number of high-visibility stocks, causing further selling, leading to a potential crash.

Insiders, for their part, have an analogous, mixed reaction to the view that the market has nowhere to go but up. Their reasons—both positive and negative—are quite different, however. As we have seen, the Insider clearly accepts the premise built into the optimistic view because there is nowhere else for money to go, that it is buying power that drives the market. Insofar as items 1, 2, 3, 5, and 6 all point to more money coming into the market, most Insiders find the optimistic scenario minimally encouraging. They tend, however, to be concerned about the quality of this buying. As long as there is sound evidence that smart money continues to favor American equities, they are likely to maintain an optimistic view. If they were convinced, however, that the really smart money had decided to favor fixed-income instruments over equity, or foreign investments over American investments, for these True Believers to change their tune dramatically. As for corporate structure and technology, most Insiders are indifferent. As noted earlier, they are really not that concerned about what to buy and sell, but rather who is doing the buying and selling.

If most Insiders are relatively indifferent to changes in corporate structure, most Cyclist-Chartists are uninterested in the entire story. For the true-believing Cyclist-Chartist, the market tells its own story, and there is no need for any other story. Talk about alternative investments, changes in the class structure or corporate organization, or any of the other items noted above is at best of secondary importance. How the market has behaved and continues to behave remains the best indicator of how it will behave.

Unlike the Cyclist-Chartists, Traders aren't interested in past market patterns but in current market behavior. For most Traders, broad optimism just makes their job that much harder. The Trader does best in markets where the mood swings back and forth, making it easier to pick out the stocks that continue to outperform and underperform the market as a whole.

Most Traders maintain an inherent skepticism toward the market that makes them question any long term prognosis. In recent years, many Traders have expressed concern about the way the general optimism has allowed various types of information to be reframed in questionable ways. One specific example of this is how many companies have been able to report higher earnings because they have treated a significant loss as a one-time, special write-off rather than being forced to include the loss in their earning statement. As one Trader stated to me, "I begin to wonder, how many years in a row is it legitimate to take a special write-off while claiming increased earnings?"

Efficient Market adherents exhibit a similar skepticism toward sweeping generalizations on where the market is going, but they clearly have benefited from the general positivism that has characterized the market through most the 1990s. Moreover, the increased participation of the public, especially the growth in pension funds and mutual funds, has served to strengthen their confidence in their own strategies. Since, unlike all the other True Believers, they are not in the business of picking one stock over the other, their success is tied to the overall success of the market. Though philosophically they are committed to the philosophy that there is no way to outguess the market, the view that the market is likely to continue to rise for broader political and economic reasons has a very attractive ring to it.

This leaves us with the Transformational Idea adherents. Of all the True Believers, they alone seem to be most taken up with the broad, optimistic scenario presented above. For most of them, however, the one item that legitimates this scenario above all others is the emergence of new computer, pharmaceutical, and biological technologies that continue to offer exciting new investment opportunities. There are those who also buy into the whole "new world" vision of free markets and capital transformation. It should be noted, however, that it is difficult to determine if it is the substance of these stories that lies behind the enthusiasm or whether Transformational Idea adherents simply like upbeat, Transformational accounts. My own judgment is that it is the latter case.

That most True Believers don't buy into the view that the market has nowhere to go but up should not come as any big surprise. Nearly all True Believers are market professionals who see the market as a complex place. Simple, one-way stories are not apt to sell very well. It is rather the salespersons of the market who are more likely to embrace this global overview. Here again, this makes sense, since the salesperson's objective is to sell stocks; nothing helps this more than generating an overall, upbeat mood. Even most salespersons, however, realize that what goes up normally comes down and that no market can or will continue to rise indefinitely. The only people left to embrace this view fully are lay investors, who do so more out of their own need to reassure themselves than out of any grounded understanding of how the market works. Here again, this should come as no surprise. Blind faith, like deep cynicism—

even when accompanied by a rationale—is an alternative to knowledge rather than a product of knowledge. This helps explain why neither the cynicism of a Henry Geller nor the faith depicted in this section characterizes our True Believers.

It also explains why such cynicism and faith normally don't characterize market salespersons. Many, if not most, salespersons might be willing to proclaim a deep faith in the market as part as their sales approach, but this does not mean that they actually accept such a view. Not that many salespersons have their own thought-out views of the market to insulate them against cynicism and blind faith as do True Believers; instead, they have concrete objectives. To put the matter quite crudely, whether the market is going up or down may be the major concern of both True Believers and individual investors, but it isn't the major concern of most salespersons. Their concern is making a sale. Obviously, they would much prefer their customers to make money rather than lose it, but the sale is the thing. As long as they generate sufficient commissions, they can live with an up or down market.

The fact that neither True Believers nor salespersons tend to embrace either the cynicism of Henry Geller nor the blind faith exhibited by many in the market does not mean that faith and cynicism are not common to the market. Indeed, most investors exhibit each mood on different occasions. It may take a Henry Geller to be a cynic all the time, but most investors and even more than a few salespersons can become quite cynical when the market turns against them. Similarly, even the most experienced investors and hardened salespersons find it difficult to control their ebullience in a market that seems to double every few years. And yes, True Believers can be overcome with cynicism or blind faith on occasion. What is fascinating is that even though such attitudes are nearly always driven by despair or euphoria, they tend to be framed in terms of the various overviews presented earlier. There is, in short, an almost compulsive need to explain such feelings in terms of some sort of coherent story of how the market functions. What that story should be, or even if it holds together, is really not the issue. What is the issue is that there should be some explanation.

Through our analysis of both True Believers and salespersons, we have seen the critical role played by various market overviews. Ironically, the importance of such accounts is probably nowhere more evident than in situations where, in fact, they cease to play a significant role. I refer here to situations where nothing seems to make sense, and knowledge, action, cynicism, and faith give way to what can only be called foolishness.

15

FOOLISHNESS: FOLLOW THE CROWD

Nearly everyone who has written anything about the market has in one way or other acknowledged the "crowd syndrome" of the market. It is an undeniable fact of market life that entraps even the most sophisticated professional now and then. In its milder forms, it appears as a "fad"; in its more extreme forms as "panic." It can emerge in an up market or a down market, but whenever it appears and whatever its form, its essential character remains the same. Everyone starts to play follow the leader, and the leader is screaming, "I must find out where my people are going, so that I can lead them."

Nearly everyone realizes that getting caught up in such a movement is madness. Nevertheless, every year nearly everyone gets caught up in one or more such events; they become Followers. Why this should be so is another question. Several different hypotheses have been suggested—emotional contagion, group pressure, and repressed anger among others—but most prove fairly superficial upon analysis.[48]

Under normal conditions, people act in reference to specific goals and objectives and according to specific rules. The goals and rules vary, and the actors may themselves be only faintly aware of what they are. The process is admittedly complex, and there exists considerable disagreement among "experts" as to the exact nature of the process. Nevertheless, there is general agreement that most human behavior is rule governed.

This raises the question of where the rules come from. Most theorists assert that the rules are built into our view of the world in which we live. We generally act as if we lived in an "ordered" world. The specific nature of this order is in turn determined by the perspective or overview that we use, which is generally determined by a wide range of cues that we receive from others. This is what is meant by the common notion that man lives in a social world. We do not give meaning to the world as individuals but rather as members of specific social groupings.

Though we engage in this process of "defining the situation" continually, it is anything but simple. It entails reading the cues of others, giving off cues ourselves, and a complex process of negotiation. In general, all of this occurs without our being conscious of what is going on. Nevertheless, the process requires that the participants "believe" that there exists some shared meaning that they can potentially grasp. There are times, however, when it becomes difficult or even impossible to know what is expected in a particular situation; we are unable to tap into these "shared meanings." When this occurs, the most common response is to "bluff it." We look about us at others who apparently know what is going on and attempt to mimic their behavior. As the saying goes, "When in Rome, do as the Romans do."

What happens, however, when no one knows what is going on and everyone is playing follow the leader? The answer is what is known as "mass behavior." Everyone acts as others are acting rather than in a rational way—in other words, they're acting not in accordance with specific goals and in response to some ordered view of the world. Despite this herd mentality, seldom does everyone end up acting exactly the same way. As one person changes his behavior to adjust to what he sees others doing, others are adjusting their behavior in response to what the first person had been doing. As a result, the most common outcome is what could be called the "milling crowd" syndrome— everyone adjusting to everyone else without any overall pattern of behavior emerging.[49]

There are times, however, when an overall pattern will emerge and the milling crowd will become a mob. All instances of joint behavior are, of course, not mobs; there are times when joint behavior is due to shared beliefs and/or coordinated efforts. These instances, however, are not characterized by the irrationality and impulsiveness associated with mass behavior, which results from the lack of governing rules.

Mass behavior most commonly occurs as a result of a breakdown in social organization—when accepted beliefs are breaking down—but it is also likely to occur in situations where there is a lack of accepted beliefs to begin with, or when there is no overall order to any beliefs. It is specifically this latter condition that characterizes the market. The very number of different market theories creates what is basically an ambiguous, unordered situation The market is consequently always vulnerable to mass behavior; there are times, however, when it is more vulnerable.

Usually, despite the lack of any sort of overall "meaning" to the market, most investors act in a meaningful manner. They stick to their own views of the market, or to the views of professionals who are advising them, and manage to ignore the other, conflicting views. This continues as long as their views seem to be working—if they are not making money, at least they are not doing any worse than anyone else is. If they get hurt, however, and lose faith in their own views of the market, they are likely to be ripe victims to the dynamics of mass behavior. And the less committed they are to begin with, the easier it is for them to lose faith.

The fact that persons in the market are constantly exposed to opposing views is also relevant. Even the most committed of True Believers know that there are other views. They confront them daily. Consequently, when they get hurt in the market, they are likely not only to doubt their own market philosophies but also to wonder if the other guys aren't perhaps right.

These factors manage to clarify one of the most paradoxical aspects of the market: namely, that the very commitment to make sense out of the market—to discover the mind of the market—often leads to what could be called the "mindless" character of the market. The instances of mass behavior that are so common in the market would be less likely if the participants attributed more to simple chance and luck. If the general view was that those who were doing very well were simply lucky, it is unlikely that a substantial portion of the not-so-lucky would blindly join in. True, there would always be some who would try to ride with the "hot hand"—those who apparently had luck with them at the moment—but it is doubtful that their numbers would be such as to generate mass behavior. But most participants simply don't believe that it is luck that is at work. It is their belief that the market has some sort of meaningful order, which leads them to conclude that those who are doing well must "know" something.

There is still the question of: "So what?" If your view of the market isn't working, what is wrong with going along with the crowd? If things turn sour for the crowd, at least you will be in good company. There are times when there is nothing wrong with this approach. In fact, if you join the forming crowd early enough, you can do well just by riding the momentum of the crowd. Unfortunately, the probabilities are that you will not be drawn into the crowd until it has already developed a good head of steam, which means that you'll be joining it later rather than earlier. This approach in the long run can spell disaster. First of all, the major move will already have occurred; second, you'll find it nearly impossible to extricate yourself from the crowd once you are in it.

So why should this be so? If everyone is bullish on the stock, why doesn't it stay up in price? The answer usually given is that, though a crowd is right in the beginning, it is wrong in the end. It is right in the beginning because the crowd generates new buyers. Many people may already have bought the stock, but there will be many more who have not. As these others join the crowd, they will push the price of the stock up further. Eventually, however, all who are vulnerable to the pull of the crowd will have bought the stock and there will be no one left. When this happens, the only direction left for the stock to go is down. Moreover, it is likely to do this very rapidly since, once the balloon has been burst, everyone will want to get out as fast as possible. Those who have joined the crowd later rather than earlier are likely to have to sell for less than they paid.

Now, there is nothing really wrong with this explanation, but it tends to oversimplify and even misrepresent the actual process. It is based on the view that stocks go up when there are more buyers than sellers and down when there are more sellers than buyers. The actual process is more complex than this, especially as it relates to market panics, whether in buying or selling.

There are never more buyers than sellers or more sellers than buyers. For every buyer there must be a seller, and vice versa. It takes two to transact. If there is only a buyer or only a seller, there is no trade and, consequently, no price movement one way or the other. It may be argued that the common beliefs regarding the ratio of buyers to sellers refer only to those willing to buy and sell at or near the present price of the stock in question. Ironically, however, if we switch our focus from those willing to sell or buy at the present price to those willing to do so near the present price, just the opposite relationship holds to that which is commonly assumed. Stocks go up when there are more sellers nearby and down when there are more buyers nearby. In order to understand why this is so, it is necessary to look more closely at what it means to be a buyer and a seller.

There are always two groups of buyers and two groups of sellers: those willing to buy or willing to sell as the stock moves up, and those willing to buy or willing to sell as the stock moves down. (We will ignore those willing to buy and sell at the present price since, in and of themselves, they will not account for any stock movement.) The catch is that only those willing to buy the stock as it moves down can be considered serious buyers now, since those supposedly willing to buy the stock as it moves up could, if they wanted to, buy it at its present price. Similarly, only those willing to sell the stock as it goes up can be considered real sellers now, since those supposedly willing to sell at a lower price could likewise sell now if they wanted to. Those persons who talk about buying a stock as it moves up and those who talk about selling their stock if it moves down are only potential buyers and sellers. Furthermore, in most cases they are only willing to be a buyer or a seller providing the stock moves in such a way that they can buy or sell at a price near the "old price."

Let us assume that a particular stock is trading at 20. The bid/ask is 19⅞ to 20⅛. There is someone who owns the stock who is willing to sell it at 20⅛ and there is someone who does not own the stock who is willing to pay 19⅞. One can be considered a potential buyer, the other a potential seller: each is thinking about it. More specifically, the first person is thinking, "If the stock acts well—begins to move up—I think I will buy it if I don't have to pay more than 20⅛." The second person is thinking, "If the stock starts to act badly—it begins to move down—I think I will sell it providing I can get 19⅞." If the first person finds out that he will have to pay 21, he may very well no longer be interested in buying; similarly, if the second person finds out that she can only get 19, she may no longer be interested in selling.

This situation explains one of the paradoxes of the specialist's book—the record the specialist in a stock keeps of potential buy and sell orders. The book contains primarily buy offers below the market and sell orders above the market. Admittedly, it also contains stop-buy orders—orders to buy a stock if it goes up to a certain level—and stop-loss orders to sell if the stock goes down to a certain level; but such orders are fewer in number than the normal buy and sell orders. You might think that many buy orders below the market was a bullish sign, since it indicates support for the stock, and that many sell orders above the market was a bearish sign, since it indicates a heavy supply. In fact, just the opposite is true. Stocks move in the direction of the orders. The fact that there are orders to buy the stock if it goes down makes it possible for the stock to go down. Similarly, orders to sell the stock as it goes up make it possible for the stock to go up. If there are no buyers just below the market, few people who own the stock will be willing to sell it; similarly, if there is no stock for sale just above the market, there will be few people willing to buy it.

Admittedly, all of this sounds counterintuitive, but it makes sense if you try to understand it in the context of the market. The person willing to sell his stock slightly above the market may be nervous and skeptical about the value of the stock, but still may see the stock as likely to go up in the short term. The person willing to buy a stock as it moves down, on the other hand, may believe in the long-term value of the stock but that it will go down in the short term. To put this a slightly different way, orders to sell a stock above the market reflect a degree of skepticism in a bullish environment, whereas orders to buy below the market represent confidence in a bearish environment. One only finds significant orders to sell above the market when the market is moving up and significant numbers of buy orders below the market when the market is moving down.

The above analysis also helps to explain why some stocks that move up rapidly stay up, yet others eventually collapse. Furthermore, it sheds some light on the market aphorism regarding "good buying" and "bad buying," "strong hands" and weak hands."

When the crowd is buying, it is the cooler heads that are selling. As long as there are enough cool heads who are willing to provide stock, the stock is likely to go up. When the crowd owns all the stock, there is no one left to sell. When that happens, the stock has peaked. Usually, there are still plenty of people out there willing to buy, but they are not willing to pay any price. It must be remembered that no one in the crowd thinks of himself as a fool. There are limits even when playing follow the leader. It is at this point that the aggressive members of the crowd take over.

Throughout an upward movement of a stock, there will always be those who will follow behind, people who will be bidding below the market. As long as there are persons willing to sell their stock slightly above the market to the more aggressive buyers—those willing to pay an extra ⅛—the presence of these followers is not felt. When the cool heads are gone, however, the followers are there, waiting to provide the down stairway for the stock. Their optimism is as necessary for the decline of the stock as was the skepticism of the original owners. That is, these latecomers now make it possible for the stock to decline.

The situation with those stocks that maintain their advance is quite different. In their case there is usually some "rational" reason for the initial move. The crowd view, insofar as it exists, is normally that the upward move is not justified. Those playing follow the leader begin to sell; it is the cooler heads who are buying. Eventually, even these stocks will peak out, but—providing a new crowd hasn't formed that now believes the stock will never stop going up—most who now own it will want to own it even if its rapid upward movement should cease for a while. Furthermore, since the crowd view would still be that the stock is, if anything, overpriced, there is not likely to be heavy demand for the stock below the current market.

It is, admittedly, seldom as simple as all this, but the underlying premise that stocks are more likely to go up and stay up if they are moving into "strong" hands, but to go down eventually if they are moving into "weak" hands, is usually valid. What it indicates about "strong" and "weak" hands, or "good" and "bad" buying, is also true. A strong hand is one that may be willing to sell at a higher price but unwilling to sell at a lower price. A weak hand is one that is usually afraid to sell at a higher price, but more than eager to sell if the stock begins to decline.

This same analysis also explains why it is a market truism that stocks will nearly always "close the gap." If a stock for some reason "gaps" either upwards or downwards—if it trades at a level significantly different from its last trade—it will usually in the near future retrace its movement to fill in the gap. A stock, for example, that jumps from 22 directly to 27 is likely to retrace its steps back to near the 22 area before it is able to continue its upward movement. The same pattern would hold true if it were to drop from 22 to 17.

The reason for this is that in the case of the upward movement there will be those who missed it at 23, 24, 25, and 26 and who will bid for it below the market, and in the case of the downward movement there will be those willing to sell it if it recovers to 18, 19, 20, or 21. They might have to wait a little while, but sooner or later their impact is usually felt.

It would be wrong and misleading to end this discussion without pointing out that the so-called strong hand is not always the hand of "big" money or the institutional investor; neither do all the "weak" hands belong to individual investors. Despite what our paranoid apologist Henry Geller says, it is not the amount of money one has to invest, it is the attitude that governs the investment. Anyone playing follow the leader, no matter how much money they have, is a weak hand and represents "bad" buying.

Though the crowd syndrome of the market is primarily due to the ambiguity of the market, there is another factor at work that deserves mention, namely, the emotional pull of the market. This might seem to introduce a new element fairly late in the game, but it has, in fact, been implicit in the argument from the very beginning.

While this summation is basically correct, it is the emotional pull of the market that explains why so many people are willing to play follow the leader. It explains why participants confronted with ambiguity don't just retreat from the whole market. Most True Believers do so when they no longer feel confident in their own point of view. The question then is, why doesn't everyone? The answer quite simply is that they don't want to. They want to be part of the excitement of the market; they get a kick out of the market that they are unwilling to give up. For most, it is like being at a large party where they don't know anyone or what is going on, but they don't want to go home.

As might be expected, the great majority of these "partygoers" are not market professionals; they are rather lay investors. This does not mean, however, that market professionals are immune to the emotional pull of the market. Remember how Harry Silver, despite being a managing partner of a very prestigious firm, still responds to the emotional pull of the market? This pull, being part of the public, is the thing he most likes about the market. Most market professionals are not as addicted to this aspect of the market as Harry Silver, but few are immune to it. Though True Believers are least likely to be pulled along, it is a rare True Believer who has never succumbed to the magnetism of the crowd.[50]

Although the foolishness of the crowd is a constant presence in the market, it is more evident at some times rather than at others. Its historical calling card has been market volatility. It is a rare gyrating market—a market that rushes ahead one minute only to collapse the next, or vice versa—that isn't being moved to a large extent by some form of crowd behavior. One could similarly argue that the final moves entailed in most major market tops and major market bottoms are products of crowd foolishness. The market surge and crash of 1987, for example, was accompanied by more than a 50 percent increase in volatility over the preceding year and the average of the previous half dozen years.[51] The years 1997 and 1998 also showed a significant increase in volatility compared to the preceding six years, though not at the level of 1987.

The jump in volatility in recent years has, of course, been attributed to other causes as well. One such cause, which has been targeted by a number of people, has been the introduction and reliance upon what is called program trading. To understand why they have been so targeted, it is necessary to explain briefly how these programs work, which also requires explaining in some detail the role of futures and other derivatives.

Trading programs differ in a number of ways from each other, but most attempt to profit from price discrepancies in the market. Such discrepancies exist when, for example, the price of a stock future is out of line with the price of the stock itself. The specifics in any given situation can become quite complex, but the principles are fairly straightforward. The value of a future—a contract to buy a particular stock at some specified future time—is theoretically based on the present price of the stock, its volatility, the length of time the future has yet to run, and the cost of money.[52] Under normal conditions, the market itself tends to price most futures in close accordance with their theoretical values. When the market moves up or down rapidly, however, discrepancies often arise. The goal of most trading programs is to profit from such discrepancies by buying the undervalued item and selling the overvalued one. When a stock starts to fall sharply, for example, futures in that stock, being higher risk issues, may lose value even more rapidly. If this occurs, it would make sense to sell the underlying stock and buy offsetting futures. Such actions, of course, cause the underlying stock to continue to fall even more.

Such strategies have existed for some time. What makes program trading different is that the entire process—recognizing that there are discrepancies, selling the stock, buying and selling the futures—is done automatically by a properly programmed computer. The computer will continue to buy and sell as long as the discrepancies exist, which generally exacerbates the move. Another factor that increases the resulting volatility is the amount of money that may be entailed. Since the projected return from most of these trading programs is set—these programs do not attempt to make money on a particular market move, but rather to generate a fixed return on a perceived price discrepancy—substantial sums of money that have been invested in fixed return instruments can flow into the market, causing significant disruptions.

Because such trading programs tend to exaggerate dramatic moves in the market, new rules have been instituted to prohibit their implementation when the market moves more than 2 percent up or down in a trading session.[53] Such restrictions do not prevent individual traders from attempting to do the same thing—many day traders do try—but they cannot rely on computers to implement either the calculations required or the buy and sell orders automatically.

The key question in the present context, however, isn't whether such programs should be allowed or not, but whether they embody another form of crowd behavior. Insofar as such programs tend to accentuate sharp moves in the market by "piling on," they would appear to mimic crowd behavior. There is an important difference, however. Such programs are not governed by the principle of following the leader. The programs don't elect to buy or sell stock because others are doing so. The programs' decisions are based on discrepancies in the market caused by such dramatic moves, not the moves themselves. Whereas the crowd is apt to buy or sell whenever the market takes off in one or another direction, trading programs will be triggered only if such movements create discrepancies. In short, they do not reflect the foolishness of abandoning all strategies that characterizes crowd behavior. They are rather the embodiment of particular strategies.

We began this study with a typical small investor trying to make some sense out of the way the market determines value. From there, we set out in pursuit of the mind of the market. What we have found is that this mind takes many different forms and operates in different ways. For a small minority of True Believers, there is an understandable logic to the way the market works. Unfortunately for most small investors, not only do they constitute only a decided minority on Wall Street, they also don't agree with each other in what this logic is. The salespersons of the market meanwhile are more than willing to use the rhetoric and explanations of practically all of the True Believers to sell stocks, but few take any of these accounts to heart. We have found others who have responded to the market with cynicism, and others who have been content to participate on faith. After all of these variations, we have discovered that many, if not much, of the most dramatic moves of the market are apparently governed by what can only be called a "mindless" foolishness. Though we clearly have not managed to determine a single, integrated account for how value is defined on Wall Street, we have managed to shed light here and there on the process. We have, for example, examined fairly closely a number of different types and their associated views of the market; we have also observed how the various types fit together and merge into each other.

We have also done something else. By examining the complexities of how value is defined on Wall Street, we have revealed a good deal about how value and meaning are determined in general. In short, though the sociology of knowledge can illuminate a good deal about how the market functions,[54] the market itself provides for us a remarkable site for understanding how value and meanings are constructed.[55] It is to these issues that we now turn.

PART V

PUTTING IT ALL TOGETHER

16

THE MARKET AS MENTOR

Three major themes run through this book: (1) the interpretive, flexible nature of the market; (2) the dominating and pervasive influence of basic market philosophies; and (3) the importance, as well as the similar and different uses, of these market overviews for True Believers, Salesmen, Cynics, Faithful, and Followers.[56] To recap:

I began my analysis by underscoring the ambiguity of the market, noting how the same "facts" can have completely different meanings to different people. I pointed out that the problem is not a lack of interpretive schemes, but rather a surfeit of such schemes due to the peculiar, responsive character of the market—that is, the extreme, "self-fulfilling prophesy" potential of the market. More specifically, six basic overviews or philosophies were introduced: the Fundamentalist view, the Insider view, the Cyclist-Chartist view, the Trader view, the Efficient Market view, and the Transformational Idea view.

The Fundamentalist view relies on economic factors: earnings, book value, price/earning ratios, and all the rest of the nitty-gritty. The Insider view emphasizes sponsorship and supply and demand. The Cyclist-Chartist view follows the past patterns of the market. The Trader view focuses upon what is called the "life," or perhaps more accurately, the emotions of the market. The Efficient Market view subsumes elements of all of the views but claims that all of these factors are discounted in the prices of stocks at any given moment. The Transformational Idea view stresses the role of new ideas and concepts.

As embodied in the views of their respective True-Believer spokesmen, these general overviews entail a number of other things as well. The Fundamentalist view defines the market as a given, external, physical reality, governed by "objective," external laws; the market is conceived of as controlled—in the long run if not the short run—by economic factors that reflect their own causal logic. This view sees nothing mysterious about the market. Anyone who is willing to work at it can find out what is going on and can thereby master the market. It is a question of work, not luck. This pragmatic attitude is revealed not only in statements bearing on what the market is, but also in the types of criticisms that the true believing Fundamentalists make of others, namely, that they were lazy, too emotional, dreamers, and the like.

In emphasizing sponsorship and supply and demand, Insiders define the market in much more interpersonal terms. The market is seen in terms of people, coalitions, decisions, and connections. This emphasis upon interpersonal relationships is aptly reflected in the major criticism that Insiders are likely to make of anyone, that is, that he or she is dishonest. Furthermore, in attempting to assess critically a piece of information, an Insider is more likely to try to see if such action makes sense to him than to look for nonpersonal supporting data.

Let's contrast the two approaches with a concrete, if hypothetical situation. If told that a large fund was planning to make a major purchase of a company, a Fundamentalist would likely review the economic fundamentals of the company to see if there had been some developments that explained the purchase. The Fundamentalist would not hesitate to call the company and to purchase shares of the company if the fundamentals supported such an action, without much concern for what the fund actually did or didn't do. An Insider who heard the same rumor, in contrast, would likely try to see if such a purchase made sense given the assets, objectives, and particulars of the fund in question. An Insider might also try to check it out through contacts, going very slowly in order not to spread the word too soon. It must be remembered that the Insider's strength is in knowing how to handle information, not just in obtaining it—knowing what the "smart money" is going to do because such buying can and will "move" the stock in a company once people learn about it. An Insider's job is to learn it first and take a position before the move occurs.

In contrast to both Fundamentalists and Insiders, Cyclist-Chartists are almost mystical in their approach to the market. Keeping charts does not make one a true-believing Cyclist-Chartist. One must also believe that the market is governed by what could be called a transcendent ordering principle. This concern with a meaningful order is revealed in the way Cyclist-Chartists see other market participants. They see them as basically ignorant; moreover, they see them as generally unable to learn even if they want to: they lack the necessary intellectual/spiritual ability.

The Trader not only sees the market primarily in terms of its own life force, but also revels in it. Of all the True Believers, none approaches the Trader in the level of "love" of the market. The Trader relates to the market not only cognitively but also emotionally. As far as the Trader is concerned, it is impossible to master the market without tuning into your emotions, though you cannot expect to survive unless you can control your emotions. To give just a brief example of what I mean here, I should like to recount how one Trader responded to my question, "How do you decide whether to hold on to a stock or to sell it?" He answered, "I imagine doing both and end up doing what feels better."

Efficient Market adherents have elements of the four previous types, or more accurately accept aspects of these types, but they are most like Fundamentalists in embracing the view that the market is normally controlled by underlying economic factors. Moreover, they generally also share the Fundamentalist's basic reason for being in the market in the first place, namely that the return on stocks in the long run will outperform the return on bonds. Unlike the true Fundamentalist, who believes it is possible to discover and evaluate such underlying economic factors before the market does, the Efficient Market adherent believes that it is pretty much impossible to do so. As a result, you can't really expect to beat the market. It is in the end a sophisticated knowledge that leads to a basic fatalism. (The Efficient Market enhancers try to have it both ways, agreeing with other Efficient Market adherents that it can't normally be done, but siding with the Fundamentalists that it is possible sometimes to improve your choices just a little bit.)

The Transformational Idea adherent is in many ways the complete opposite of the Efficient Market adherent. True-believing Transformational Idea adherents, like Efficient Market adherents, are familiar with all of the various theories of the other True Believers. (To be fair, all True Believers are familiar with the views of the other True Believers.) Like Efficient Market adherents, and unlike other True Believers, Transformational Idea adherents also tend to believe that it is impossible to out-think the market when it comes to tracking the various factors upon which the other True Believers rely. Rather than surrendering to the market, which is in effect what Efficient Market adherents do,[57] Transformational Idea adherents put their trust and money in the transformative power of ideas. In doing so, they reveal a similarity with Cyclist-Chartists, who also rely on what could be called symbolic forms. Whereas Cyclist-Chartists seek to discover these forms in the market itself, Transformational Idea adherents seek their ideas in industry, commerce, and changing lifestyles.

Having analyzed these various True Believers, we switched our attention to the various ways they are used by salespersons to sell stocks and examined the ways these same views are used to support the explanations offered by both Cynics and the Faithful. In both of these cases, however, the objective was not to guide action or to influence others, but rather to justify what has been done and/or will be done. In the case of the Cynic, this generally means doing nothing; in the case of the Faithful, it means holding on.

Finally, we attempted to show how the very richness of these various views, the surplus of explanatory accounts, could lead to confusion and foolishness as embodied in crowd behavior and the crowd syndrome, which in turn tends to generate extreme volatility. In summary, though the form and mix vary, our analysis of these other market styles showed that the market is continually defined in terms of the basic philosophies of the True Believers.

As informative as all of this has hopefully been, it has failed to answer two very basic questions: (1) Why these overviews? and (2) Why True Believers, salespersons, Cynics, Faithful, and Followers? We have not dealt with these questions because my principal concern has been with presenting an integrated picture of how values are assigned and what the mind of the market looks like. In painting this picture, my focus has been informed by theory and has often touched upon these basic "why" questions, especially the first. It is now time, however, to deal with them directly, if briefly—to locate each in terms of what may be called our common sense grasp of different forms of "knowing."[58]

The first overview (the Fundamentalist) is associated with our natural attitude toward the external, physical world, that is the world of objects, causality, rational means/ends, order, and external "giveness." The second (Insider) is related to our world of interpersonal relationships—other wills, relationships of dominance and submissiveness, mutual understanding, and argumentation. The third (Cyclist-Chartist) connects to our symbolic universe of meanings per se, where the criteria of conceptual order (consistency, coherency, completeness, harmony) reign supreme, whereas the fourth (Trader) is based upon our world of "sensual" experience, with its pain and pleasure, emotive tone, and either/or tendencies. The fifth overview (Efficient Market) incorporates all, but its highly deterministic stance clearly mirrors that of the Fundamentalist. The sixth view (Transformational Idea) shares the Cyclist-Chartist's emphasis on meanings, but whereas the Cyclist-Chartist sees meanings as providing order, the Transformational Idea adherent sees meanings as change agents.[59] Without stretching things too far we could say that the first and fifth appear to reach their highest form in modern science, the second in law and legal systems, the third and sixth in religion and philosophy, and the fourth in art.

The market offers us an excellent opportunity to compare these different overviews and the tone of each. In the market we can clearly see the "rational" bias of the economic—and efficient market—overview, the "conspiratorial" bias of the political overview, the "compulsive and ideational" bias of the ordering and transformational overviews, and the "intuitive" bias of the market action view.

Initially one might attempt to deal with the second question (why these various styles?) by asserting simply that that is the way things are. As an historical fact, this is exactly the way I approached these various styles even after I was well into the study. I might add that I found them an irritating empirical fact of life that was complicating an otherwise fairly straightforward presentation of different market philosophies. I finally accepted them as part of the market and left it at that. Insofar as I bothered to question why someone elected to be a True Believer, Salesman, Cynic, Faithful, or Follower, I assumed the answer to lie primarily in their relative success early in their careers. True Believers did tend to be more successful than all others except for a few Salesmen, and Salesmen tend to make more money if not do better in the market than Cynics, Faithful, and Followers.

Further thought and re-analysis of my notes and interviews revealed that there was much more to it than this. It showed that True Believers, Salesmen, Cynics, Faithful, and Followers as groups approached the market differently— had different objectives—just as those who favor different market philosophies framed the market differently. It was not just a question of how well they had done but also a question of what they expected from the market and consequently how they saw the market. This, in turn, determined what they accepted as the objective and function of an understanding of the market.

At the risk of venturing into some pretty muddy water, let me state that how and what an individual accepts as the purpose and function of knowledge is not the same as the individual's own purpose. Nearly everyone I have ever met in the market was interested in making money in the market. Furthermore, nearly all were interested in getting along with the people they dealt with, in understanding what was going on, and in enjoying themselves as best they could. However, to return to where we began, True Believers, Salesmen, Cynics, Faithful, and Followers differ in their views regarding how an understanding of the market relates to these other objectives.

True Believers seek to understand the market in order to master it, which means in order to make it work for them. A True Believer is intent upon making money in the market, and on doing so in terms of a return on capital. A True Believer will take a salary and commissions, but the objective is capital gain. This is true not only of the Fundamentalist but also of the other True Believers. The final test of any idea is the extent and degree to which it allows one to master the market. It does not matter how smart the persons think they are; if they know what they are doing, they should be able to prove it by the money they make. Moreover, they should be able to do so with minimal risk.

Salesmen, in contrast, use their knowledge of the market to impress and influence people in order to make sales. They seek to establish some sort of consensus with their customers while at the same time maintaining their position of expertise. They see and use knowledge primarily in a social-psychological manner—as a tool to aid them in interpersonal relationships—rather than as a means for gaining mastery over an external, nonhuman world. As we saw earlier, this is most clearly the case with the Customer Salesmen, but it holds true for the other types of salesmen as well.

For both Cynics and the Faithful, meanwhile, the purpose of market knowledge is to provide them with an account that serves to make sense out of the market; they want to believe that there is some sort of underlying order to the market. Some, like Henry Geller, may take a cynical view of this order, whereas others prefer to be more optimistic. Whether upbeat or downbeat, they—like nearly all ideologues—much prefer that the sense they seek be simple. In short, the key function of market knowledge to both Cynic and Faithful is that it provides a clear view of the market.[60]

This leaves us with the Followers and the crowd syndrome. What function do the various overviews of the market have for them? The answer, I feel, is quite clear. The various explanations and accounts that the Followers grasp at as they are pulled along provide them with a sense of belonging, a sense of solidarity with others. The Follower does not want to master the market, influence people, to search for "meaning." The Follower wants to be part of the action and is hooked on the same social dynamics of the market that Traders like John Holland and Action Salesmen use to their advantage. For the Follower, however, the goal is to belong by sharing whatever passes for knowledge with the others in the crowd.

In summary, we can see that the same dimensions used to classify the basic overviews of the market can be used to classify the way these overviews are used. This is graphically represented in the matrix in Figure 1. In addition to giving us a picture of the various market types described in this study, this

Figure 1. Matrix of Stock Market Types

Interest Stressed
In How Overview
* Is Used*   *Interest Stressed in Overview*

	Economic/ Instrumental	Political/ Interpersonal	Ordering/ Ideational	Libidinal/ Expressive
Economic/ Instrumental	**Fundamentalists and Efficient Market Adherents**	**Insiders**	**Cyclist-Chartists and Transformational Idea Adherents**	**Traders**
Political/ Interpersonal	**Firm Salesmen**	**Customer Salesmen**	**Market Salesmen**	**Action Salesmen**
Ordering/ Ideational	**Cynic/Faithful Economic Fatalist**	**Cynic/Faithful Conspiratorialist**	**Cynic/Faithful Ideational Fatalist**	°
Libidinal/ Expressive	**Greedy Followers**	**Insecure Followers**	**Confused Followers**	**Natural Followers**

°There is a natural antipathy between these two parameters, resulting in few if any investors fitting this description. This explains why the cell is empty.

chart allows us to understand better a number of apparent paradoxes. We saw earlier, for example, that even relatively successful, true-believing Insiders often end up in sales, and that similarly successful, true-believing Cyclist-Chartists often end up as explainers.[61] We also saw that though it is possible for a true Fundamentalist to go along ignoring everyone else, a good Trader must keep a hand on the pulse of the crowd. We similarly saw how many successful Firm Salesmen can become almost indistinguishable from true Fundamentalists, whereas even the most competent Action Salesman often appears to be nothing but a player. All of this could be accounted for by a general pull toward what could be called intentional homogeneity—a tendency to define the world in a manner that is consistent with the purposes to which we put this knowledge. The reverse of this is also true, namely that there is a tendency to use knowledge in a manner that is consistent with the basic modality of the knowledge itself.

In terms of the matrix in Figure 1, what this means is that we should expect there to be a pull toward the shaded cells. There is evidence to support this view. Among True Believers, Fundamentalists tend to dominate. The most successful salespersons are Customer Salesmen. The situation with the Cynic, Faithful, and Followers, however, is more ambiguous. It is probably true that the Natural Follower is most likely to get caught up in the mass psychology of the market, but that would appear to be a tautology built into the matrix. The Cynic and Faithful create other difficulties, with Cynics like Henry Geller often favoring a conspiratorial view and many Faithful a positive, economic, deterministic view. For the great majority, however, my hunch is that their cynicism or faith reflects a deeper cynicism or faith regarding life's meaning in general.

To talk of the different uses of knowledge in the market is one thing; to attempt to generalize from the market is quite another. It is a truism, for example, that people get involved in the market for all sorts of reasons, such as the money or the excitement. Consequently, it does not seem to require any great stretch of imagination to accept the idea that people are apt to perceive the market quite differently, and that they are likely to use whatever knowledge they have of the market in different ways. Can one, however, generalize from the market to other spheres of social life? I firmly believe that we can, and here I refer not only to the basic overviews and their respective intentional dimensions, but also to the inherent "rationalities" of these overviews and their various uses.

At the race track, for example, some bet on those horses that appear to have the best record of past wins or bloodlines. They could be called race track Fundamentalists. Others like to follow what they consider to be the "smart" money, usually the large bets that come in just before post time. They would be our race track Insiders. Others—our race track Cyclist-Chartists—look for clues in the particular number assigned to the horse, the day of the week, or some other series of numbers with which they are familiar. And there are yet others—our race track Traders—who bet in accordance with their own instinctive response to the animals as they parade in front of the grandstands before the race. Finally, there are those—our race track Efficient Market adherents—who believe that there is no way to select winners, and those—most similar to our Transformational Idea adherents—whose bets are determined by some governing idea.

There are some, of course, who prefer to own horses and race them rather than to bet on them. There are others who prefer to take the bets of others, and then there are those who write how other people should bet. Finally, there are those who just like watching the horses run. Similar examples could be presented describing the way people approach and deal with almost anything from a work of art to a crystal dug up from the ground.

There remains, however, one final and very important question. What, if anything, does the market tell us about the relative priority of these various modalities, "logics," and uses of knowledge? Can we say that one orientation, one logic, or one purpose is more basic than the others? Or why one orientation, logic, or purpose is selected over the others? Does the market, for example, shed any light on the controversy among the different outlooks: those who argue that the purpose of mind—human reason—is to reveal the structure of the external world, and that hence knowledge must be judged in terms of this external reality (the instrumental view); those who argue that mind functions primarily to establish and maintain social order (the interpersonal view); those who argue that mind is essentially concerned with its own internal order and structure (the ideological view); and those who see the prime function of mind as providing very special grounds for human solidarity (the expressive/socially symbolic)?[62]

What our analysis of the mind of the market indicates is that it is useless to select one orientation, one logic, or one purpose and to ignore the others. It indicates that the market's mind is inherently multifaceted and that any attempt to deny this will only lead to an incomplete picture of whatever subject is being studied.

Though this conclusion is basically negative in tone, it tells us what not to do; it carries with it an implicit positive injunction as well: to give greater emphasis to human reasoning's social nature. It does so in two ways: (1) accepting reason's multifaceted character, in effect, means to give greater emphasis to its social character, since it is specifically this aspect of reasoning that is most commonly ignored; and (2) acknowledging this multifaceted character entails placing reasoning within a social context, because it is only in such a context that the various aspects of reasoning can be meaningfully integrated. Our analysis of the market would seem to suggest a third reason, that the constant pull of the crowd indicates that social solidarity may indeed be the primary objective of human reasoning.

The market, of course, remains a fairly unique and distinct place. One must consequently be careful in making too broad generalizations about life in general. Nevertheless, I find it as difficult today as I did twenty years ago to disagree with John Holland's statement, "The market is one of the best models of life that you are likely to find." I say this today, however, with considerably more mixed feelings than I did twenty years ago. I say it with more enthusiasm insofar as the market itself has become more self-reflexive. Sociologists for many years have argued that social reality is to a large extent a social construction, that the reality we confront is to a large extent a product of our own making. Whereas twenty years ago, most people approached the market as if it

somehow existed in and was a product of purely physical forces, nearly everyone today accepts its socially constructed character.

At the same time, I am also more troubled. Twenty years ago, I didn't worry
about anyone making the market into an icon to be emulated. In light of the
present enthusiasm and fascination for the market, I feel compelled to point
out that, though the market might mirror life in general, it remains a very
partial image. Even more troubling is the fact that, as limited as the image
might be, the stereotypical way in which the market is commonly portrayed is
even more circumscribed. The real market is not the sterile market of neoclas-
sical economics, but a rich world of overlapping and conflicting accounts and
self representations. So to those eager to buy into John Holland's characteriza-
tion, I feel compelled to add another well-known market adage: "Buyer beware."[63]

PART VI

SOME PRACTICAL ADVICE FOR THE INDIVIDUAL INVESTOR

BASIC CHOICES FOR EVERY INVESTOR

I began this book by quoting the market aphorism, "The only thing clear about the market is that nothing is clear." I also noted that the reason for this was that different persons defined the market differently. To everyone in the market, none of this is news. They do not have to be told that the market is confusing, nor that they are confused. Most, in fact, are not only confused but also worried. The descriptions of the various market philosophies and the various types may help to explain the problem, but it certainly doesn't resolve it. There remains the question of what an investor is to do.[64]

There are a number of answers to this question. Three of the most common are: (1) get out; (2) get someone else to manage your money; or (3) try to master the market.

For many years, the simplest path appeared to be simply to get out of the market. During the sixties, seventies, and early eighties, few who took this option regretted it, especially if they had locked up high interest rates on fixed securities. Since the mid-eighties, however, this hasn't seemed to be a wise choice.

And there are other reasons, unrelated to what the market has done, that make the first option questionable. In a nutshell, it seldom works. It doesn't work, because the reasons for people becoming involved in the market in the first place—the desire to make money, to be part of the action, to relieve boredom, whatever—just do not go away. In fact, for most the desires become greater; to make matters worse, most also feel that if they were to go back, they would be able to do better than last time. (It should be understood that most who leave do so having done pretty badly.)

It might be argued that it doesn't matter how one gets out as long as one gets out. But it does matter. The person who is forced out, even when suppos-edly making the decision, is always vulnerable to be sucked back in. Here one might counter, "Burnt once, twice shy," but as we have seen the market is more subtle than this. "There is more than one way to skin a cat" and in the market, each approach represents a potentially new way to "skin the cat." I could cite innumerable examples to support this claim. Here are three.

Don Young is in his mid-fifties. He is a successful cardiologist and has already quit the market "for good" three times, the first time in the mid-seventies. For eight years, he had maintained an active account with an Action Salesman. During those years he owned scores of stocks. Some did well, some poorly. After eight years, however, he had only slightly more than when he had started, and he had been adding money each year. After two particularly bad trades, he had a fight with his broker—he called him a crook, among other things—and cashed in his chips. He told me then that he would never go back to the mar-ket. "All those guys are croupiers. I'd do better in Vegas."

For close to six years he was good to his word. In the early eighties, however, he began to take a different position. It wasn't the market that was so bad, but the broker he had had and the approach he had used. In fact, Don had con-cluded that it wasn't even wrong to speculate. The secret was to limit one's losses. Through a friend he had been introduced to a broker in Texas who had worked out an almost foolproof way to make money by selling covered options. By 1985 he was fully invested again. To make a long story short, by the begin-ning of 1987, he had quit the market again "for good." "I can't believe it," he told me. "I must have owned at least six stocks that nearly doubled, but because of the options he had sold I made less than anyone else I know." Given that he then put most of his money in three index funds, he didn't complain when the market took off in the nineties. He does miss the action, however. My guess is that he will be back again.

Sam and Esther Higgens are both now deceased. They were in and out of the market from the late twenties through the mid-eighties, and their historical facts are somewhat different, but the end results were very similar. They first got involved in the market in the twenties. In the crash of '29 they got hurt—not that badly, but enough to convince them that the market was no place to put their hard-earned money. In the late forties, however, they decided to give it another try. This time, they promised themselves that they would be more careful. For close to ten years, working with a fundamentally oriented broker, they maintained a very conservative approach. They made money. Unfortunately, they didn't make nearly as much money as a lot of other people. In the late fifties, they had an argument with their broker and switched their account to a broker who was more oriented to trading. Again they made money, but again they ended up having a fight with their broker over a specific trade. They sold all of their stocks and put their money in a savings bank. I had an opportunity to talk to them during this period, and they were adamant that they would never invest in the market again. They were convinced that all brokers were crooks. Two years later, however, they were back in the market. This time they were seduced by an apparently very successful broker who had access to a lot of very good, "inside" information.

Helen Andrews first got involved in the market when she bought a computer stock on the advice of her boss. He had some "good" information on a small West Coast company with which he did business. The situation worked out and she nearly doubled her money—about $5,000—in three months. For the next three years, she followed one tip after another. In the process she doubled her money again—only to lose half of it in a single, two-week period in one stock. In disgust with herself and her broker—who was her boss's broker—she got out of the market in 1994. By 1996 she was back in again; moreover, she was with the same broker and following the same approach. When questioned about this she told me, "Well even with my losses I still was ahead. I guess that if I want to make money I'll have to learn to take my losses in stride."

Many people who get out of the market have historically got back in by letting someone else manage their money, usually by buying in to an actively managed mutual fund. Unlike investors who work with their own broker, most who invest in actively managed mutual funds have given up trying to make sense of it and turned that responsibility over to someone else. Unfortunately, the results—as far as making money is concerned—are not much different from the results achieved by those who reinvest for themselves. Often they're worse.

One case that comes to mind is that of Mr. and Mrs. Williams. For over twenty years, they played the market. During this period they switched brokers a number of times. They never, however, quit the market—even during bad periods, and they had a number. They didn't, in fact, really even ever give up on their brokers. Each switch was due more to external circumstances—such as a move or an introduction to a new broker—than to their frustration with the broker that they had at the time. In fact, after more than twenty years in the market, both felt fairly confident in their own abilities to manage their own money.

With retirement, things changed. The contacts and flow of information upon which they had based most of their investment decisions began to dry up. This was followed by one particularly bad year, 1977, in which they lost more than 20 percent of their assets. As a result of these developments, plus their desire to travel more extensively, they decided to sell all of their stocks and to invest in an actively managed yet conservative mutual fund. After eight years with this particular fund, their net assets were less than they would have been if they had bought corporate bonds. During the next ten years they did considerably better, but the S&P index outperformed their fund by more than 100 percent. Others have had similar experiences.

The problem with most actively managed mutual funds is that professionals are generally no better at mastering the market than the nonprofessional. As we have seen, most professionals are subject to the same vagaries and conflicts as the individual investor. Moreover, no one manages someone else's money for love. The professional has to make a living, and takes the cut off the top. Consequently, in order for a mutual fund to do as well as the market as a whole, it must in fact do better.

Despite these drawbacks, it would seem reasonable that at least some funds should be able to do just that. Some do. Unfortunately, it is pretty much impossible to tell ahead of time which managed funds will do well and which will not. Just as some stocks will always outperform the market, so will some funds. Some investors attempt to adjust to this situation by trading funds. The "up-front" commissions charged in the purchase of many mutual funds, however, make this nearly always a losing proposition. Even in the case of no-load funds, few people can expect to make money by adopting a short-term trading approach.

Some funds, however, should consistently outperform the market. Here I have in mind funds managed by a True Believer of one sort or another. Historically, most small investors have had access to such True Believers only by investing in some fund or other. And some funds such as Warren Buffett's clearly have outperformed the averages. Unfortunately, such funds are relatively few and often difficult to get into. Moreover, even the most successful money managers have been exposed recently to pressures that have diverted them from their original objective. They are being judged more and more in terms of the money they have under management than by their market performance per se.

On the surface this might not appear to represent any sort of conflict. Excellent performance would seem to be an excellent way of acquiring additional investments. Investment decisions, however, aren't generally made on performance per se, but rather on relative performance. As a result, money managers must base their investment strategies not only on their analysis of the market but also on their analysis of what other investment firms are doing. They are not out to do the best they can, but to do better than the others. This change occurred when money managers began running institutional accounts. It was the institutional investor who first evidenced a desire to beat the competition, rather than the small investor, whose primary objective remained that of making money. Nevertheless, the small investor got caught up in this development, like it or not, since even the most market-oriented money managers know that their own jobs depend more upon the amount of money they have under management than upon how well they do with that money. Investment decisions, therefore, are often determined with an eye toward future sales of the fund as much as by an eye upon the actual performance of the portfolio. Moreover, there is a fear in some cases of outperforming the competition too much, since this may lead to the judgment that such a fund entails a higher degree of risk than funds whose performance better mirrors that of other funds. One particularly astute money manager once complained to me that he was actually afraid to outperform the competition "too much": "A few years ago, if I doubled my money while everyone else did 10 percent, I would have been a hero. Today, if I did the same thing, I'm more likely to be accused of taking unnecessary risks and actually lose accounts."

(Though this view was expressed by more than one money manager whom I interviewed, I must admit that I still find it somewhat difficult to accept at face value. I think that most money managers are more concerned with keeping an eye on the competition than they were, but I can't help feeling that most would still be very happy to outperform the competition significantly even if this meant that they stood out and could be accused of being too speculative. Whatever the real situation, most money managers feel a greater need to project an image of soundness as well as an image of brilliance.)

As a consequence of these developments, even if an individual investor is fortunate enough to pick a fund managed by persons capable of mastering the market, the probabilities are that fund managers will be unable to perform up to their full potential. For the individual investors the bottom line is that their chances of beating the market by having their money in an actively managed mutual fund are not any better than they are dealing with a competent retail broker.

So where does this leave us? What is the individual investor to do? Here, there appear to be two answers: (1) Don't attempt to beat the market; simply go with it by putting your money in a few high-quality index funds.[65] (2) Learn to manage your own account. It is possible to mix the two approaches. By and large this is the advice that one is most likely to get from reading any of the numerous books published for the individual investor. For most it is even good advice. Unfortunately, it is also advice that is difficult to follow over time.

The first step of putting your money, either some or all, into an index fund usually comes quite easily. The problem is leaving it there when the market begins to move sharply either up or down. When that happens there is a great tendency to get out, put more in, or some combination thereof. Unfortunately, moving funds in and out of an index fund destroys the very purpose of such a fund. One way to insulate oneself from such temptation, especially if you follow the market, is to split your resources and put some into an index fund and manage the rest yourself.[66]

This is where, for most people, things go from difficult to nearly impossible. The problem is that understanding the market is a full-time occupation; few have the time. This becomes obvious when you begin to examine what is required: an understanding of how the market itself works, the strategies and style of one's broker, and—last, but not least—one's own interests and objectives. Here it may seem that I am overstating the case, but let us look at what is actually entailed in such a project.

To begin with, an individual investor has to start by familiarizing himself or herself with the "market basics." The best place to start would be the local library or bookstore. Though many of the hundreds of books that have been written on the market are not worth reading, there exist a few with which all serious investors should be familiar. My three favorites remain Graham and Dodd's *Security Analysis,* Gerald Loeb's *The Battle for Investment Survival,* and Adam Smith's *The Money Game.* In combination, these three books provide a good basis for an understanding of the market; updates of the first also provide bibliographic references to a number of other books for those willing to do additional reading.

The next step would be to spend some time with three or four of the more popular financial publications. If I had to choose three, I would pick the *Wall Street Journal, Barron's,* and the financial section of the *New York Times.* Anyone with leanings toward the Transformational Idea approach would be well advised to include the *Investor's Daily*. Later, if there is time, one could also look at such publications as *Business Week, Forbes,* and *Fortune.* It would not be enough to read one or two issues; unlike the books mentioned earlier, these publications do not pretend to give a general view. They focus on current news. If they are to be of assistance in developing an overview of the market, they must be digested over a period of time. It would probably make sense also to learn how to surf the Net and locate a few market-related Websites that one finds useful.

Time. The word was used three times in the last paragraph. The fact is that it requires a significant amount of time to acquire even a superficial under-standing of the market. From my own experience, I would say that you would have to plan on an initial investment of at least fifty hours and a continuing investment of between ten and fifteen hours a week. Must one put in this time? Regarding the first fifty or so hours, I would say yes; regarding the ongoing ten to fifteen hours a week, I am less dogmatic. It would be possible after doing your homework for a period of months, or whatever time is required to develop a general idea of what is going on, to cut back on the weekly assignments. This would, of course, make you more dependent upon your broker. If you have a good broker and if your time is limited, this would not necessarily spell disaster. But it does mean that you would have to know your broker better than would otherwise be the case.

"Know your broker!" Few rules are more important to the individual inves-tor. Unfortunately, most people know next to nothing about their brokers. They may know where they live, how many children they have, their clubs, if they are a Democrat or a Republican, but few know anything about their brokers' market philosophy or market style. Considering how hard most people work for the money they invest, this is hard to believe, but it is true.

How do you begin to determine the market philosophy and style of your broker? To begin with, you would have to have some familiarity with the vari-ous major overviews of the market, as well as major types of brokers. This present study could provide the grounds for such knowledge. You would also have to have a general understanding of the market itself, which this book and those mentioned above could also provide. All of this, however, would merely be background knowledge; you would still have to come to terms with your own broker.

How could you do this, given that the various types are often difficult to distinguish from one another? It is difficult for market professionals and social scientists to distinguish between similar types; the problems for most lay investors would be greater since they have the added problem of trying to separate their brokers' true views from those projected as part of the image. Fortunately, the individual investor has an important option, an option that too few ever use: Ask your broker to spell out his or her views. You must, of course, know the questions to ask.

You would have to ask your broker all of the following questions: What types of stocks does she prefer her customers to own? Asset-rich companies? Blue-chip companies? Growth stocks? Market leaders? Or does he have certain specific companies that he likes to follow? How important does she feel institutional investors are in determining the direction of the market? Is he worried about stock manipulation in any specific situations? Does he believe in market cycles, and if so, do these cycles primarily affect the market as a whole or individual companies and industries? Does she give much weight to market timing? What books would he recommend that you read? What periodicals should you keep up with? What does she read? Does he subscribe to any advisory service? How important is the tape to him? Does she follow it regularly? Does he give much importance to any technical indicators such as the "put/call ratios," advance/decline ratios, or other sentiment indicators? What does she think of most institutional research? What does he think of his own firm's research? What is her attitude toward the use of options? If he thinks they are useful, it is important to determine whether he believes only in selling covered options, or whether he is willing to "go naked" or to buy options. What is his attitude toward using margin? Does she prefer her customers to diversify their holdings, and if so to what degree? What percentage of your assets does she believe should be in the market? What other types of investments would she recommend? What does he think of his fellow professionals? Do most of them know what they are doing? How sophisticated does he believe his own customers are? How does she conceive of your mutual responsibility in making market decisions? Does he enjoy being a broker, and, if not, what would he prefer to be doing? Finally, how does she feel about investing her own money in the market? If she does invest, does she also trade?

Obviously, you could not hope to ask all of these questions in one sitting. You would have to plan on giving this project a considerable amount of time. There would still be the problem of knowing what to make of the answers. You would have to determine two things: (1) to what degree the broker is a True Believer and to what degree a salesperson, an explainer, or just a follower; and (2) which is his or her market orientation. The points discussed earlier would be of some help in doing this, but it should be clear that neither job would be very easy.

If you were successful in doing these things, the probabilities are very high that you would discover that your broker was a salesperson, not a True Believer. Her primary concern would not be to master the market, but to sell stocks. You could attempt to find another broker who was a True Believer, but I am afraid the possibility of being successful would not be very great; there are just not that many True Believers, and only a minority of them manage retail accounts. This would not necessarily mean failure any more than finding a True Believer would mean automatic success. It does mean that you would have to be very selective in following his advice; you would have to be able to distinguish advice honestly given and a sales pitch. In nearly all cases this requires setting firm limits on the types of information you are willing to accept. On the positive side, the average salesperson, because he is more eclectic, allows the individual investor to follow an investment strategy that may be more in keeping with the investor's own orientation than would most True Believers.

To make the best use of your broker, you would have to begin by determining which orientation she is most comfortable with. This can usually be done by analyzing the answers to the various questions above. Taken as a whole, the answers should indicate with which approach the broker feels most comfortable. Since she is unlikely to be a True Believer, she will not be wedded to one approach. Nearly all brokers, nevertheless, have their own strengths and weaknesses. Firm Salesmen, almost by definition, are more secure when dealing with stocks recommended by their firm; Customer Salesmen are usually better at evaluating market stories. It should be remembered that all brokers would like their customers to do well; it is clearly good business, and thus for the most part they try to do their best. It is up to the investor to know what this "best" is. If and when she begins to push a stock for reasons different from those she normally gives, it is time to be on one's guard.

Does this mean that you can follow your broker with confidence provided he is consistent? No! It must be remembered that the expertise of any salesman is that he knows how to sell. By forcing him to stay with what he knows, one would only insure that the broker would be playing his strong suit; in any suit, however, there are good and bad cards, and the broker normally knows which are which. If you the investor let your broker know that you are not only willing but prefer to wait for the right card, you will more often than not force the broker to be more selective than would otherwise be the case.

The effect of following the procedures outlined above would only insure that you would get the best possible service from your broker. It would still be the broker, however, who would be making most market decisions. This raises the question of whether there are other rules that would allow the individual investor a greater say in making market decisions. The answer to this question is yes; for the average investor, however, such rules are of little use. Any rule is only valid as part of a general market approach. Unless you are willing and able to put in the time required to develop a proprietary market approach, which few are willing or able to do, it is usually counterproductive to try to second-guess your broker when it comes to the particulars. It is a case where a little bit of knowledge can be a dangerous thing.

This doesn't mean that you as an investor should take a completely passive role in the management of your account, but in order to take a more active role you would also have to know yourself. This may seem like strange advice, since most of us feel that we know ourselves quite well. It must be remembered, however, that I am talking about a very specific type of knowledge. I am talking about knowledge of market philosophy and market style. Few investors have any knowledge of themselves in this regard. They may have some idea of the amount of risk they are willing to take and the amount of return they desire, but what of their general views of the market? Do they see the market in terms of supply and demand, or in terms of underlying economic values? Do they feel that the market is inherently ordered, or is it governed primarily by chance?

These questions are of fundamental importance to those investors who want to manage their own accounts; the answers should serve as the foundation for developing a market philosophy. They are also important for those who are content to rely upon their broker because the broker-customer relationship is a social as well as an economic relationship. Whatever the ability of the broker or the customer, the relationship will not work unless there is trust and some degree of empathy. I am talking here about market empathy, not personal empathy. The most successful True Believer will seldom make any money for a customer if the two are not in sync. If the broker is a Fundamentalist, the customer will become bored and sell just before the long anticipated move; if a Trader, the customer may panic at the wrong moment. In contrast, it is often possible to make money with a moderately astute salesman when your market rhythms are in harmony.

To know with what you are comfortable and what you can take is perhaps the most under-rated element within the market. It best explains why so few people are able to follow their own advice. Anyone who attempts to trade, for example, learns very quickly about the need to limit losses, yet there are few who are able to take the "short loss." Similarly, Fundamentalists continually stress the need for patience, yet many are unable to exhibit it. The fact is that there are no universal rules; each style has its own rules. The secret is to find a broker whose basic style is compatible with yours.

In light of the three-part program just outlined, it should be clear why few persons could even consider it as an option: most people simply do not have the time. Even if they did, I would guess that most would find the whole process disagreeable. It would be one thing if success were guaranteed, but knowing what we do of the track record of even the few True Believers of the market, we know this is not so. The possibility of making money in the market following option 3 is definitely better than following options 1 or 2, but it remains a possibility, not a certainty.

Given this situation, it is not surprising that many hopeful investors become frustrated. Fortunately, the very difficulties described above create another, somewhat esoteric option, which I label "cutting loose." In its simplest terms, to cut loose means to avoid being seduced by the crowd.

18

AVOIDING THE CROWD

Initially, it might appear that it should be relatively easy to cut loose. All that is really required is to avoid the crowd. This, in turn, just requires ignoring all the nonsense that you hear, which should not be too difficult since most people recognize it as nonsense to begin with. In the concrete reality of the market, however, cutting loose is much more difficult than it would appear.

First of all, the crowd is not that easy to recognize. Yes, there are times when you can almost hear the panic in your broker's voice, when you can see the jump in volume, when you are hearing the same thing from everyone. In most cases, however, the crowd is much more subtle. There is little evidence of panic; the changes in trading activity are not that dramatic; and not everyone is in agreement. Your broker is not telling you that you "have" to do anything; just that he feels you should. There may be a general mood to the market, but it is not a ruling passion. It may be seductive, but it is definitely not coercive.

You could avoid even these subtler crowds by ignoring everything that you hear. Such an approach would carry its own costs. But by cutting loose, I don't mean picking stocks by throwing darts in your basement. Any "rational" approach to the market requires information of some sort, and even the most astute investor can benefit from some sort of advice. In short, it is generally impossible to be "in the market" without being "in it."

Cutting loose also doesn't mean never going with the majority. The majority is often right, at least for a period of time. The problem comes when you surrender your judgment to that of the crowd. It's fine to act in concert with others, but continue to think for yourself. The rub is that thinking is itself normally a social process that incorporates others.

So what can you do? Begin by doing some of the same things that those who want to be students of the market do. First, I would advise putting a significant portion of your funds in a few highly capitalized index funds. Second, in order to manage the rest of your money generate some personal, coherent view of the market. It can be a relatively simple one, and it need not conform to that of any specific type of True Believer. It must have a degree of logical consistency, however, and be capable of producing certain rules of market behavior. It does not matter what the rules are, as long as there are some rules.

The need for some set of rules is essential; without them you are lost. Some rules, of course, are better than others. The key, however, is to have rules that can be applied in practice. You should have some rules, for example, regarding the types of stocks you want to own. Such rules can refer to the price-earning ratio of the stock, the industry involved, a particular product you like, its yield, its price range, or any of a number of qualifiers. The specifics are not that important. What is important is that you are able to ask yourself if the stock in question is the type of stock you would like to own. In this regard, it is also useful to have a few rules regarding types of stocks that you do not want to own.

Next, it is a good idea to have some rules on when you are willing to buy and sell a stock. Again, it does not matter that much what the rules are as long as you apply them consistently. You might decide that you only like to buy a stock when it has made a new high, or when it has gone down 25 percent or more. Similarly, you might decide that you like to sell a stock when it has gone up, or down, 20 percent, or after you've owned it for six months. Completely separate from any decision regarding stock selection, you might discover that you can only pick winners when you have surplus cash. The key point again is not how good the rule is but that it is a rule.

To say that it doesn't matter what the rule is may sound silly. Obviously, some rules must be better than others. Remember, however, that the purpose of these rules is not to make you a sophisticated investor. If you want to try that route, go back to the advice given earlier to those willing to become students of the market and put in the time required. The purpose of these rules is to protect you from being seduced by the crowd. The function of the rules is not to guarantee success but to avoid disaster.

Once you have managed to put together a set of basic rules, the next step is to take a good close look at yourself. This same advice was given to those planning to become students of the market. If anything, it is even more crucial for the less committed investor. Part of this self-examination should deal with your own attitude toward the market—how you see it, what it means to you, and the like. You will already have started this process in formulating your rules, but it is useful to push these types of questions further than the rule information process itself requires. More important, you should work to judge your own emotional relationship to the market. For the "casual" investor, this is more important than the self-knowledge that bears on market philosophy per se.

What does it mean, however, "to judge your emotional relationship to the market"? Are you a nervous investor? Are you always afraid that your stocks are going to go down? Or do you tend to be too complacent? Do you sit back quietly as your stocks go down, telling yourself that they are bound to recover sooner or later? How greedy are you? Are you happy with a 10 percent return, or do you expect to double your money? Do you like it when your stocks are on the most active list, or does it make you uncomfortable? The purpose of all of these questions is to enable you to have some idea as to when you are likely to be most vulnerable to the pull of the crowd, which in most cases will be when you are uncomfortable.

Once you have done these things, you should be ready to confront the market itself. Here, you must remember four things: (1) that the market is characterized by a number of different philosophies, (2) that most brokers are salespeople, not market experts, (3) that the market as a whole is always susceptible to mass psychology, and (4) that while you want to make money, the major thing is to avoid getting wiped out.

With all of these points in mind, now it is time to set limits on the types of information you are willing to receive. You will obviously need and want some types of information and even advice, but most of what is offered you will not want. The specific types of information and advice that you will want will depend upon the rules you have set for yourself and what you know about your own strengths and weaknesses.

For example, if you have decided to limit your investments to low price-earning ratio stocks, you do not want to hear about any high flyers—no matter what your broker or your brother-in-law has heard. Similarly, if you have decided to sell any stock that declines by 20 percent, you don't want to know that a big mutual fund has started to buy the stock. If your broker continues to give you such information and advice after you have told her not to, get a new broker.

You should expect, however, to be told those things that you want to hear. If you are very conscious of yield, you want your broker to tell you if there has been an announcement of a dividend increase. Similarly, if you have told your broker that you don't like buying stocks that sell for less than $10 a share, you want him to remind you of that fact when you tell him that you are thinking about buying a $5 stock.

It is very possible, if not probable, that by doing this you will ignore some good advice and be talked out of some sound investments, but you will also be protecting yourself from getting involved in situations that you are not capable of handling. Keeping a check on your own emotional state is more difficult. Self-analysis doesn't work very well under the best of circumstances; in the market, with its high emotional tone and the need to make rapid decisions, it is often useless. It is hard to tell, when the adrenaline is pumping, if you are nervous because you are afraid that the stock that you own, which has gone up 15 percent in two days, is going to give it all back tomorrow, or whether you are greedily waiting for it to double within the week. Nevertheless, there are some precautions that you can take.

One of the best is to play "if, then" games with yourself. In the example just given, try to sit back for a moment and ask yourself, "How will I feel if I don't sell it and the stock collapses tomorrow and gives back its move?" Likewise, "How will I feel if I do sell it and it doubles within the week?" In both cases, you'll probably not feel very good, but it is likely that you will feel like kicking yourself more in one situation than the other, because in that case you'll feel like you should have "known better." You will have gone against your own rules, no matter how ambiguous they might be.

Such "if, then" games can and probably should be played before taking any action at any time. It is amazing how often one discovers things one didn't expect. You might be thinking about buying a company, but aren't particularly enthusiastic. The thought of it going up and you not owning it, however, makes you very angry. Here, your emotional response has served to make you apparently "unemotional," but the "if, then" game would reveal what is really going on. In another situation, you might find yourself champing at the bit to buy a certain stock, but when you compare how you would feel if you missed the move to how you would feel if the situation didn't work out, you might discover that you'd be more upset if the situation didn't work out.

It would be nice if it always worked out so nicely, but it doesn't. There are times when it is impossible to get a reading on yourself even after playing such mental games. There are times when both options make you feel like kicking yourself—just as there are times when you could live with either option. In the latter case, it generally doesn't matter what you do; in the former, you are better off getting out, or avoiding getting in. You are simply off-balance and vulnerable for a fall.

The need to avoid acting when you are off-balance has other applications. You are likely to be most off-balance and hence most vulnerable after taking a reverse or having made what you consider to be a mistake. This can occur in a number of different circumstances: the failure to buy a stock that proceeds to double; sitting with a stock that collapses; failing to take profits on a speculative run-up, and many others. The examples are many; moreover, most people know, after the event, when they have made a mistake and when they are hurting. What they often don't recognize is the extent to which their next decision is influenced by such reversals.

I can remember one experience many years ago, when I had sold a stock too early. It had had a good move and I was nervous, so I sold it though it had shown no evidence that it was about to collapse. Three days later it continued its upward movement—without me—and I sat there kicking myself. Without really realizing what I was doing, I then proceeded to take the money and invest it in another situation that I had not really been following. It wasn't a bad investment—in fact, I made some money from it—but it was not of the same quality as the one I had sold out of. Nevertheless, what I did was a mistake and it cost me much more money than I made. As things turned out, three days later the original stock had a two-day correction, during which time it came back to about the area where I had sold it. In terms of the overall action of the market it continued to be a standout; in short, it was a buy. Unfortunately, I didn't have any money left since I had, in a rebound action, put it all in the other stock. I could not sell the stock I had just bought because it wasn't acting badly either. So there I was, locked out of the one stock I should have owned.

It could be argued that I should have sold the stock and bought back into the first stock. In hindsight maybe, but even forgetting the extra commissions I would have had to pay, the fact of the matter is that I was off-balance and I knew it. Anything I did was likely to be a mistake. Rather than giving myself a little time to regain my equilibrium, I had acted hastily, with the result that I ended up more off-balance than I had been three days earlier.

From what has been said, it should be clear that the act of cutting loose does not mean becoming a contrarian. There is obviously some similarity to the two postures, but they are not the same. Each is intended as a means of avoiding the crowd, but in most cases the so-called contrarians constitute a crowd themselves, or at least their actions are controlled by the crowd almost as much as if they were part of it, though admittedly in reverse.

The logical flaw in the contrarian's position is that it focuses attention upon the action of the crowd rather than on the crowd itself. As noted earlier, the crowd may be right; in fact, in the beginning it usually is. To try always to go against the crowd is the same as always trying to go against the tide, and that makes little sense. There is nothing wrong with going in the same direction as the crowd provided that you are not part of it and that you can control your future actions when the crowd goes off in another direction.

In point of fact, most so-called contrarians are not that contrary to begin with. Given the nature of the market—everyone normally going in different directions—it is pretty difficult to determine the dominant mood. On the same day that I have been informed by one self-anointed contrarian that he is buying, I have been informed by another that he is selling. The only way to avoid getting caught up in a crowd is to maintain your own counsel, to be true to yourself and your own rules of market behavior.

I have already touched on some of the reasons why this is so difficult. There are all of these conflicting views that generate an ambiguity, which nurtures mass behavior. There are also all of those salespersons pushing you this way and that, to say nothing of one's own greed and fear. And there is another factor at work: Despite claims to the contrary, the market tends to create an image of itself that makes joining the crowd not look that bad. At times it even makes it look comforting if not actually wise. It may be a case of giving people what they want, but it has its own effect nevertheless.

This might seem to be a cheap shot, but look at the image that the market, or rather those persons running the market, project. Merrill Lynch is "Bullish on America!" And what image do they give us? American industry at work? No! A herd of steers running along together. They don't even give us a good bull. And then there was the E. F. Hutton's "What does your broker say?" "Well, my broker is E. F. Hutton (which, of course, was not true since his broker was really either Al, Fred, or Mary) and E. F. Hutton says . . ." followed by everyone trying to hear what E. F. Hutton has to say.

Even something as innocuous as the "most-active list" feeds into this syndrome. For some (primarily Traders), the most-active list is of central importance. For most, it has little if any real importance. Nevertheless, it is always on prominent display. In fact, the market is always playing up the crowd and suggesting that if you get with the "right" people and/or the "right" stocks you'll be okay. I am not saying that this is the intent, but it is definitely part of the effect. The market, of course, is not unique in this respect. We are always being seduced to follow the crowd in one way or another. This is why the advice to be "true to oneself" is just as valuable in the market as elsewhere.

FOUR RULES FOR SUCCESS
AND SURVIVAL

At the risk of oversimplifying things, I think it is time to get a little more specific, though it is impossible to lay down specific market rules that will work for all people at all times. Different strategies require different rules. Nevertheless, there are I believe, four that nearly everyone should attempt to follow. There is nothing "holy" about them in and of themselves; their purpose is to aid you in following the more general advice presented above—namely, to be true to yourself, to think for yourself, and most important, to avoid being seduced by the "crowd." First offered twenty years ago, with slight modification they have stood the test of time quite well.

1. INVEST IN SITUATIONS THAT YOU CAN UNDERSTAND

I first wrote this more than twenty years ago. It was thus quite reassuring to find that Warren Buffett expressed the same opinion to explain why he avoided most high technology stocks despite their remarkable market appreciation. For Warren Buffett, a Fundamentalist, understanding a stock means understanding its book value, earning projections, all the details. I am more eclectic. What I mean by this rule is only that you should have some clear idea as to why you think the stock should go up in price. It may be that you believe that new management will be able to turn a company around, that you see an increased demand for a particular product, that you see an interest in a particular industry, or any of a number of factors. Your specific reasons are not important; what is important is that the reasons are your own. Only if you have an understanding of why you intend to do what you intend to do can you judge when the situation has changed and when another decision is required. In short, you must know which factors are relevant to your decision and which factors are irrelevant. As noted earlier, you don't need to be a genius to survive on Wall Street; you just have to avoid being a fool. Unfortunately, it is pretty easy to become a fool on Wall Street. All you need to do is to keep switching from one approach to another without knowing what you are doing.

2. LIMIT YOUR LOSSES

This rule is followed by all True Believers, though they formulate it in different ways. You cannot hope to be successful in the market if you allow yourself to sustain substantial losses. A 50 percent decline in assets requires a double, just to get even. Tomorrow will always offer new opportunities, but you will be unable to take advantage of them if you have nothing to invest. Furthermore, you may never regain your balance. A large loss is bad enough in itself, but more often than not it makes you vulnerable for even greater losses.

So how do you limit your losses? The simplest way is to set a limit in your own mind—let's say a 10 percent loss—and to stick to it. If the stock declines by 10 percent below your purchase price, you sell. The simplest way, however, is not always the best way. The 10 percent limit notion is in most cases too rigid. It is better to set a specific price—usually within or close to the 10 percent limit—below which you feel the stock should not fall if your initial evaluation of the situation is correct. You should have a reason for picking the price you pick. The most common, and probably the best, reason for setting a specific price is that the stock has in the past been supported at that level—in other words, it has not gone below that price in the recent past.

This technique is commonly referred to as taking a short loss. For many years, I swore by it. Unfortunately, the increased volatility of the market brought on by the growth of institutional investors, day traders, and program trading has undermined the value of this technique. Some years ago, you could expect that the specialist on the NYSE or the major market firms trading NASDAQ stocks would hold a stock above a well-defined support level under normal conditions. Unfortunately, there may suddenly be a sell order of sufficient size that a specialist or firm is unwilling to maintain the price for all of the sale. When the price drops, it is very possible that a new buyer will appear who quickly lifts the price back over the old support level, but if you have left a stop/loss order on the book, you will have been taken out of the stock. This development has not discredited the principle of limiting one's losses, but it has made it more difficult to implement. One needs to set one's sell points with some flexibility, which means that one can't play the market as closely as one might wish.

Often it is the case that you cannot find even a general support level within the 10 percent limit. If that is the case, you should seriously reconsider your original decision. The fact that a stock goes down a few points is usually not sufficient reason to sell it. You want some indication that the stock is not behaving properly, and the violation of support levels is such an indication. Beware, however, of putting yourself in a situation where you will have to sustain a major loss before such a support level is penetrated.

Once you have determined the price below which you will not carry a stock, you must stick to it within the conditions noted above. There will be times when a stock will seriously penetrate a support level and then turn around and come charging back. The probabilities are still great that the next major rush will be further down rather than up. Even if the stock doesn't collapse, there are probably better places for your money to be.

There are times when you may be fortunate enough to have two support levels within the 10 percent limit. Let's say you buy a stock at 54 with a near-term support level of 52—it bounced off 52 twice during the last two weeks—and a longer term support level at 49—49 has been the low during the last nine months. In such a situation you could play it very cautiously and sell if the stock broke the 52 level or you could hold it. If you elected to hold it, however, it would be silly to then sell the stock at 50½. Once it breaks the 52 level, your new support level is 49.

If you watch the market closely and have a good broker with whom you stay in daily contact, you may be able to follow this rule by simply keeping your "sell price" in mind. For those less involved in the market, it is advisable to take more concrete steps. The stop/loss order has been the most common way to do this, and in medium-traded stocks with good liquidity and some institutional ownership, it is a technique that can still be used. Where liquidity and volume are very thin or where stocks are subject to day traders and/or program trading, however, putting such orders on the book can be risky. I'd rather have an alert broker ready to call. The emergence of the option market, specifically put options, provides another way of handling this situation.

A put option can be looked on as a form of insurance. To use the example above, after buying the stock at 54, you could buy a 50 put option. The option gives you the right to sell the stock for $50 during the time period of the option, and would cost perhaps 1¼ to 2½, depending on volatility and expiration time. In this way you could insure that you could always get $50 back on your original $54 investment.

There are both advantages and disadvantages to using the option approach over the short/loss approach. One disadvantage is that it will normally cost you a little more in commissions. Another is that the price at which the option may be exercised will probably not be exactly the same price that you would have selected based upon past support levels. And if you buy a put option as a hedge against a stock, you cannot normally treat the underlying stock as a long-term hold. Finally, the stock you are interested in may not have a put option. On the positive side, the option route gives you much more flexibility than a stop/loss order. With a stop/loss order, once your stock has penetrated its support level you are out. With a put option, you can wait and see what happens. If the stock keeps going down—say, to 45—and your option is about to expire, you can still exercise your option and get $50 for your stock. On the other hand, if the stock goes down to 47 and then comes back to 54 or even 58, you can let it expire and you will still own the stock.

The option route allows for another alternative. Let us assume that the stock declines to 45, but that it does so as the result of a very bad market or some other factor that really has nothing to do with the stock. Furthermore, let us assume that during this decline it twice runs into major buying at the 44 level, which happens to be the low of the stock during the last three years. In such a situation, you may decide that you would like to own the stock and could sell your put option for approximately $5. That, in effect, would lower your original cost to $49. Admittedly, you would be stretching the 10 percent rule a little, but not so much as to make such a decision untenable. This is often referred to as buying down, buying a stock as it goes down. This is not a technique that I would recommend unless you really want to own the company, and unless the stock is performing better than the market as a whole.

There are other ways one can use options as a form of insurance. Anyone attempting to use options in this way, however, must make sure that they understand what they are doing, and remember what their basic objective is— namely, to protect themselves from a ruinous loss.

3. DON'T BE AFRAID TO MAKE MONEY: RIDE YOUR WINNERS

Rule 3 is really a corollary of rule 2. Just as you should not be complacent with a loser, you should not be scared of a winner. As long as you think a stock is worth as much or more than its selling price, you should hold it. But how much is it worth? That is for you to determine and brings us back to rule 1.

Unless you are only interested in income, it doesn't make much sense to buy a stock at 25 if you think it is only worth 25. You buy stocks that you think are worth more than their current selling price. How much more? Again, it depends upon your overall strategy, but for most people, given the inherent risks in any investment and the unavoidability of some losses, it makes little sense to invest in a stock unless you can see a possible 50 percent move somewhere in the near future (one to two years).

The problem for most people, and it is a problem, arises when they get 20 of that 50 percent. The tendency to grab the profits and run is very great. When this happens, you must ask yourself, "Is the stock likely to be worth more than it is selling for?" If the answer is yes, don't sell.

If the stock reaches the goals you had set, then the situation is quite different. Unless matters have changed in such a manner to make you increase your expectations (I am talking about real reasons that make sense to you, not simply the fact that the stock has reached your original goal), the stock can be sold. Similarly, if you are forced to conclude that your original judgment was overoptimistic, you may want to sell at a lower price than you initially contemplated. The key in all situations is to sell only when you believe the stock deserves to be sold, or it becomes a larger portion of your portfolio than you want.[67]

Your reasons for deciding when a stock is fully valued will depend upon the particular market philosophy that you adopt. Regardless of your reasons or what price you select, you should have a clear objective in your mind when you buy a stock, just as you should have a clear idea of what type of loss you are willing to sustain. Here, another option strategy can be useful.

From what has been said, it should be clear that I don't recommend buying a stock at 27 and selling a call option at 30. Certain traders can play this game using short-term options, but it requires more time and sophistication than most investors have. If the stock advances to the mid-30s, however, it may make very good sense to sell a 40 call option. Such an option may serve as insurance against greed, just as a put option can function as insurance against fear and/or complacency. The extra money that you will receive for the option is always welcome, though it obviously won't be much. But more importantly, it will force you to seriously reconsider your position if the stock reaches 40. Rather than ignoring what is happening, you will have to decide whether you are willing to let someone else take your stock at 40, or whether you would rather, in effect, repurchase the stock at that level by buying back your option. Whatever you decide, you must remember that the main function of the option is not to earn you a few extra dollars but to insure that you maintain some sort of rational orientation toward your stocks.

4. USE MARKET ORDERS

There are some very sophisticated investors who rely very heavily on limit orders—orders to buy or sell at a specific price. And there are situations that almost seem to demand limit orders. Nevertheless, as a general rule for most investors, "Use market orders—buying or selling at the market price" is sound advice.

Initially, it might appear as if rule 4 contradicts rules 2 and 3. Isn't a stop/loss order a limit order? Did I not say that you should set specific prices for yourself? Isn't that just what a limit order does? The answer to the first question is "no." A stop/loss order is not a limit order. Once the stop has been hit, your stop/loss order becomes a market order. (There is such a thing as a stop/loss limit order, but this is not the type of order that is being recommended.)[68] Similarly, setting a specific price in one's mind is not the same thing as using a limit order. Once your stock reaches the price you have set, you should act even if you do not get the exact price you want. With limit orders this might not happen; rather than forcing you to act, limit orders often cloud the issue and allow you to procrastinate.

Rules 1, 2, and 3 all have one basic objective: to force you to have a clear and defined idea of what you expect the stock to do, as well as a clear commitment to do specific things in response to the way the stock performs. They should also protect you from being thrown off-balance. In short, rules 1, 2, and 3 should together tell you whether a stock should be bought, held, or sold. Though limit orders can theoretically be used to support decisions arrived at in this manner, in general they have just the opposite effect. People use limit orders more as a hedge than anything else. The stock is up to 42 and you are not sure if you really want to sell it or not, so you put in a limit order to sell at 43. Or, the stock is down to 17 and you are nervous but you know that it might come back, so you put in a stop/loss order to sell at 16.

If a stock should be sold, it should be sold. A quarter of a point here or there will not change the situation. Similarly, if a stock deserves to be bought, it deserves to be bought. Orders should follow decisions; the order should not be allowed to make the decision for you. Admittedly, you can decide to sell at a specific price and enter a limit order, but as a general practice the use of limit orders has the debilitating effect of allowing you to avoid making decisions.

Are these all the rules one needs? Obviously not. They are the only rules that I know of, however, that I think can be recommended to everyone. Those interested in more specific rules that apply to specific market philosophies can find them earlier in this book. However, I have stressed the rules here because I have reached the conclusion that the mind, or rather minds, of the market is not what is of prime relevance to the average investor. He or she should have a familiarity with it, but need not master it. The investor's problem is rather the mindless character of the market that the very plurality of views tends to generate.

I could go on for pages detailing how unrelenting is the pull of this mindless character of the market, even on supposedly sophisticated investors who should know better, but, unfortunately, I don't have the time. I just heard that a major oil company is thinking about taking over a small eastern coal company that has been acting well lately, and I want to check the story out with one of my neighbors whose brother-in-law has a franchise with the oil company, before I call my broker to find out what he thinks. Thankfully, my wife has put most of our money in an index fund.

A THEORETICAL AND METHODOLOGICAL NOTE

This book reflects my four-decade fascination with, and study of, financial and auction markets. It builds on and continues the research reported in my *Mind of the Market* (1981) and *Auctions: The Social Construction of Value* (1989). Theoretically, it is grounded in what is generally referred to as the sociology of knowledge,[69] though I prefer to consider it an empirical study in the sociology of mind.[70]

The sociology of mind is similar to the sociology of knowledge in that its primary foci are the world views and common-sense perspectives of everyday life. It is further similar in that it shows how these different world views are capable of generating different "realities," which in turn can lead to different actions; it also attempts to locate these world views within a social context. Where the sociology of knowledge emphasizes the relationships among specific perspectives and specific social positions, the sociology of mind emphasizes the social parameters of thought and mind itself. In this respect, the sociology of mind has more in common with Max Weber's interest in different forms of rationality[71] and Jurgen Habermas's notion of various types of "cognitive interests."[72] That is, the sociology of mind is more concerned with forms of thought than the specific content of thought. It is, however, most definitely a sociological concern rather than a purely philosophical or psychological one, in that it sees these forms of thought as having social roots.

In acknowledging that there exists a plurality of thought forms that reflect a range of human interests, the sociology of mind underscores the complexity of human mentality. It also tends to highlight the extent to which much (even most, if not all) human reasoning is a process whereby we attempt to impose some sort of order on a world experienced as highly ambiguous. This propensity to experience the world as ambiguous and overwhelming and the consequential predisposition to impose some sort of order on it is the "catch 22" character of human reflexivity. As George Herbert Mead noted some time ago, reflexive thought transforms the simple here and now of the world as experienced through our basic senses into what for all practical purposes is an open-ended world in which what is immediately experienced can call forth images and thoughts linked to other places and other times. In short, the initial impact of reflexive thought is to greatly complicate our world. The human response has been to seek to avoid the anxiety thus generated by simplifying the world by imposing a more manageable order on it. Nowhere is this process better evidenced than in auction markets, where the ambiguity is explicit rather than tacit—price is being actively debated and determined. From a research perspective, such markets have the added advantage that their clear focus on price, rather than on a whole array of other types of values and meanings, makes the process less opaque. This is why action markets are the ideal strategic research site, noted earlier, for transforming various forms of tacit knowledge into discursive form.[73]

Though I earlier characterized this book as an empirical study in the sociology of mind, I should like to stress that the research that generated this study was neither undertaken nor pursued in order to generate empirical support for a theoretical position. It is rather a product of a genuine and long-time personal interest in the stock market. Admittedly, as a theoretically oriented sociologist, I have always approached the market with various theoretical questions in mind, but it has been the market itself that has been the primary structuring force of this study. Whatever theoretical status it may have, therefore, it is primarily an empirical study based on (1) more than three thousand hours of participant observation (by this I mean structured participant observation, not simply watching the market) carried out over a period of thirty years; (2) three series of formal interviews, numbering thirty, forty-five, and ten, respectively, with specifically selected market professionals; and (3) an ongoing, analytically critical relationship with one particular stock market professional who has served as a prime informer.[74]

I emphasize this last relationship for two reasons: first, though I established both formal and informal contacts with numerous market professionals—for example stock brokers, partners in brokerage firms, market analysts, fund managers, and private investors—none of those relationships even approached this one in terms of the amount or the quality of information I was able to obtain. Second, and more importantly, though I was fairly open regarding the nature and substance of my research with the various market people I met, talked with, and observed, I did not engage them in the types of explicit theoretical discussions that were common between myself and my prime informer.[75]

It is nearly impossible to judge the relative importance of these various sources of information. If, however, I had to quantify them, I would say that the study is based 50 percent upon participant observation, 25 percent upon formal interviews, and 25 percent upon my prime informer. There were a number of the other factors, however, that had a bearing on my ability to obtain this information and that deserve a brief comment.

Throughout my research I continually ran into four major problems: (1) gaining entry; (2) establishing trust; (3) obtaining verification; and (4) maintaining autonomy.[76]

Gaining entry is a very real problem when doing a study such as this. Most market professionals have a fairly skeptical view of social scientists. They have no good reason to talk to a sociologist or a social-psychologist; their time is worth money to them; moreover, they are not very eager to share their view of the market, which is often fairly critical, with a stranger. Most firms are even less eager to have anyone snooping around.

It became apparent very early that I could not simply walk into a brokerage firm and hope to interview anyone. I might have tried to pass myself off as a potential customer, but for professional and ethical reasons, I could not do this. Moreover, I doubt that I would have been able to get the type of information I wanted if I was seen as a potential customer. What I needed was some sort of sponsorship. When it came to interviewing institutional salesmen, management personnel, and money managers, sponsorship proved indispensable.

In order to obtain sponsorship, I relied almost exclusively on referrals from persons I had already interviewed. In nearly all cases, it was further necessary that the person referring me be either a close personal friend of the new informer or someone in a position of authority. Those in positions of authority proved most useful. In more recent years, I have been able to use a greater number of my own contacts that I have been able to develop over the years.

The number of interviews I was able to generate through personal contacts averaged between one and two. When starting with people of influence, I was able to average four or five new interviews. Consequently, I spent a great deal of time trying to develop contacts with these influential persons. I was seldom able to convert initial contacts into formal interviews—in fact, about 80 percent of the time these people were interviewing me to determine whether they would sponsor me to interview others.

In order to obtain their sponsorship, I had to convince them (1) that I was not out to cause trouble or simply to do a muckraking job on the market, (2) that I would not violate any confidences, and (3) that I knew something about the market. In most cases, I was able to relieve their mind regarding points 1 and 2 by referring them to mutual acquaintances who, more often than not, had made it possible for me to be granted this first interview. Point 3, in most cases, however, proved to be the most important criterion. It was only when I was able to show that I was familiar with the market and the way it worked that I was able to acquire new sponsorship. I was never tested in a formal way. It was rather necessary for me to prove in informal conversation that I understood the market and moreover that I liked it. I had to show that I was already a "market insider," and I am quite sure that if I hadn't been able to do this, fewer doors would have been opened to me. It almost seemed to be the case that if I already knew what I knew, no harm could come from my learning a little bit more.

The need to show that I was familiar with the way the market worked was crucial in the actual interviewing process in developing the sense of trust required if I was to get meaningful responses. Again and again for the first ten minutes to half-hour, I found my interviewees fencing with me. They would hedge their answers and ask me to explain in more detail what I was trying to do. Many would also question me as to who I was working for and what I intended to do with the information I was collecting. They wanted to be assured that everything they told me would be confidential. As I was able to show that I was familiar with what they were doing and what they were saying, however, nearly all adopted a different attitude. In some cases, this would happen after I had discussed a particular stock that the interviewee had mentioned; in other cases, it seemed to occur more as a result of the way I formulated my question—how I used market terminology.

Interestingly, once this occurred, most interviewees opened up completely. In fact, many prolonged what was basically an hour interview into a two-hour discussion. The one group that tended to maintain their reserve was the Firm Salesmen. This, I think, was primarily due to their fears that I was, in fact, working for the firm in some capacity or other. In most cases, however, I found it difficult to restrain my interviewees and so to complete my interview.

People were willing to talk openly with me, but I soon found I had a problem of verification. Many of those I talked with had a tendency to exaggerate their own success in the market and the job they were doing for their customers. In some cases, I had other contacts, often in management, that I could use for verification. Such contacts, however, were of limited use since I could not very well get up in the middle of an interview to check out what I was being told in order to insure that I was getting a true story. Furthermore, I was hesitant to use such contacts, since that would have in a way violated my commitment of confidentiality. I found, however, that the more I was able to convince the person I was interviewing that I was familiar with the market, the less likely he or she was to try to impress me. More than once, the person I was interviewing began to give me an honest story only after caught in a misstatement of some sort. A classic example of this was a broker who had originally told me that he was heavily invested in one of the market's standout stocks, only to be ignorant of the last quarterly earnings of that company. "Well, I'm really not that heavily into it. One or two of my customers have a few hundred shares." Rather than being hostile toward me as a result of such interchanges, most became even more engaging and more direct. It was as if my interviewee decided that if I knew enough to spot this dissimulation, perhaps I was someone worth cultivating.

My last problem was that of maintaining autonomy. This was not a general problem, but it did arise a number of times. On a few occasions I was approached to feed back information that I had acquired. Sometimes it was no more than a request that I give my opinion as to whether I thought the person I had interviewed would work out or not as a broker. On one occasion I was even offered the right to look over some monthly production figures in return for such information. In all cases, I refused to offer any such opinions, with the result that in one case I became persona non grata. I mention this point only because such offers are very attractive when doing a study of this sort; given the need for sponsorship, it is very difficult to turn one's back on individuals who can open doors for you. Fortunately, I had by that time established enough contacts so that I could afford to lose a few. If I had confronted such a dilemma early in my research, the temptations would have been much greater.

In summary, I found that the essential element of such a study is that one must already be very familiar with the subject matter. For some types of research, professional degrees are sufficient to open the right doors. In the case of the market, they are not, and I would guess that they are not in most situations in which one is dealing with people of influence and wealth. These people are simply not impressed; in fact, they may very well be put off. From a theoretical position, this is a known point; in practice, however, it is too often ignored.

There remains one important issue related to this study, or more exactly the evolution of this study, that should be noted for a variety of reasons. I refer to the point made in chapter 1 that the stock market has much greater visibility today than it did twenty years ago. In and of itself, this does not change anything that has been said in the preceding pages. It does, however, raise certain caution flags that I believe need to be minimally acknowledged.

In the last few years, interest in the stock market has spread not only from Wall Street to Main Street and Pennsylvania Avenue, but also to the groves of academia. In my own discipline of sociology, few fields have grown as vigorously in recent years as has economic sociology,[77] and within economic sociology, a major growth field has been the sociology of markets.[78] Even more exciting for me personally has been the increased interest in examining these markets from a sociology-of-knowledge perspective. Put slightly differently, it is widely accepted today that not only does market behavior influence how we think about markets but how we think about markets influences market behavior. This view, moreover, is not limited to academics. It is, for example, a central thesis in George Soros's bestseller, *The Crisis of Global Capitalism.*[79]

Though all of these developments have enriched both our understanding of markets and our sociological understanding of a range of social practices, I would suggest that we have only begun to grasp the full implications of these developments. More specifically, I would suggest that the increased interest in the market in recent years reflects not only the growth of the market per se but also the greater importance and saliency of market framing—in other words, seeing the world from a market perspective. Recent years have seen not only the globalization of the market, but also the marketization of the globe. This entails much more than the spread of capitalism. It entails seeing the world differently.

How? If this book has revealed anything, it is that the stock market contains a rich variety of interpretive perspectives that are themselves used in and for a variety of different purposes. Articulating these differences has been the major concern of this book. Even amid this variety, however, there are certain common themes. Of these, perhaps the most important is the general move toward abstraction and universalism. Georg Simmel made this same point some time ago in his classic *The Philosophy of Money* in which he showed how money and, in effect, monetary markets entail the objectification of subjective values.

An important related point, which is often overlooked, is that the purpose in moving beyond individualized subjective values to more universal objective values is to resolve the ambiguities inherent in individualized subjective values. It is this capacity to resolve value ambiguities and establish common pricing that is the defining characteristic of markets, especially auction markets. It is specifically this capacity, I would suggest, that explains the dramatic globalization of markets in recent years. The world is a very multifaceted entity. Markets, by filtering out and converting subjective values into prices, enable these multifaceted parts to interface with each other.

We seem here to be caught in a contradiction of sorts. Throughout this book, I have stressed how the same facts and acts are defined differently by different market players. Moreover, I have implicitly argued that this is one, if not the most important, lesson to be learned from the market. Here, however, I seem to be saying that the unprecedented growth in global markets has been due primarily to the ability of markets to fudge differences. Though this all might appear to be somewhat paradoxical, it makes perfectly good sense.

The prime function of a market is to resolve ambiguities by reducing the rich array of meanings and values that people assign to objects to a consensual price. To paraphrase a familiar aphorism, "The market can determine the price of anything, and cares about the value of nothing." How it accomplishes this transformation process, however, is far from simple. Different people use different perspectives, embodying different interests, in a variety of ways.

In this context, John Holland's comment presented at the end of chapter 16 takes on greater significance than it had twenty years ago. Although incomplete and misleading accounts of how markets functioned might have irritated some market aficionados and economic sociologists twenty years ago, the harm done was probably quite minimal. The dangers of such statements today, however, are quite real. There is nothing inherently wrong with working to resolve value ambiguities in pursuit of a consensus that can then support a wider, more inclusive exchange network. This is what Simmel referred to as objectifying the subjective. The danger emerges when these objectified values are themselves reified. We're in danger when we fail to understand that the prices so generated are themselves not only socially constructed but also constructed in a variety of different ways reflecting different philosophical positions.

This is more than a hypothetical concern. Marketization is not limited to the global economy. It is a process that flourishes at home. More and more pension plans are being made market dependent. A few decades ago, most pension plans were defined benefit plans, which meant that retirees' pensions were based on years of service; today, more and more pension plans are defined contribution plans. In these plans, retirement benefits will be determined by how well the money paid into a pension fund does in the market. In effect, this is what the recommendation to invest Social Security payments in the stock market entails. Similarly, policies governing such items as minimum wage and welfare payments are being reframed to weigh marketplace factors more heavily. It was only a few years ago that decisions regarding appropriate welfare payments and minimum wages took into account what was required to maintain a reasonable lifestyle, social equity, civic responsibility, and the like. Today, the debate is more likely to be in terms of the cost and benefits of such payments within a broader market context. Legal settlements, including alimony and child support, which were historically determined primarily in terms of factors like equity, responsibility, and societal objectives, are today more often than not decided in terms of market evaluations. Serious people argue that rather than prohibiting various types of pollution, we should sell pollution rights. Others argue that we need to allocate transplant organs through a market mechanism.

To avoid any misunderstanding, I should stress that though most of these ideas make me nervous, I am not arguing against them simply because they are based on market principles. I love markets and utilize market principles all the time. If this study has revealed anything, however, it is that markets are considerably more complex and multifaceted than one is likely to believe by reading most economics books. What is truly scary about many of the calls for society to rely more heavily on market principles is the fact that the principles cited are a parody of the principles that are actually at work in most markets. Many of our most vocal market proponents speak as if the commonly hyped market principles of rationality, maximization, level playing field, knowledgeable actors, and supply and demand somehow grasp market behavior. When they are confronted by the fact that this is not the case, many go so far as to argue that because these market principles are the "true values" of the market, we should seek to impose them on all market transactions. Somehow their conception of market principles has become the embodiment of all that is right and even moral.

Whatever their strengths, markets clearly need to be tempered by other values and rules. In this respect, I am in strong agreement with those such as George Soros and Anthony Giddens, who have argued that we need to insure that markets remain subject to civil and political objectives.[80] I must note, however, that markets tend to have their own resiliency and an ability to generate the rules and practices required to make them work as they are intended to work. They similarly have the potential to become highly self-reflexive. This has clearly been the case in most auction markets, where the rules and practices of different types of auctions have evolved differently to deal with differences among buyers, sellers, and other participants. It is presently happening on the Internet, where different rules and practices are being tested on different Websites. In short, while it may be true that "markets may know the price of everything and the value of nothing," it also seems to be true that markets, if properly managed (or perhaps more correctly, if allowed to evolve), have the ability to learn minimally what is required for their own survival. When markets fail to evolve, it is normally because they have been constrained by some purely theoretical model derived from some combination of very questionable, neo-classical assumptions. My hope is that the account of the success and survival strategies of Wall Street examined in this book will help support what I would suggest is the inherent adaptive character of markets, especially auction markets, rather an attempt to force markets into a preconceived mold. If it does, then John Holland's statement that "the market is one of the best models of life that you are likely to find" will take on new and more profound meaning.

A SELECTED GLOSSARY OF STOCK MARKET TERMINOLOGY

Account   Refers to either a specific customer or the holdings of such a customer. Many customers maintain a number of distinct accounts, such as cash accounts, margin accounts, short accounts. See also *discretionary account* and *street account.*

Account executive   Label used for a stockbroker by some firms and individuals; may be applied to both retail and institutional brokers.

Accumulation   Describes the process whereby supposedly large, sophisticated investors, usually institutional ones, are buying a particular stock over a period of time. Normally considered to be a "bullish" sign for the stock. See also *distribution.*

Acquisition   When one company takes control of another company, usually through a transaction that includes a stock offering or trade of some sort.

Action   Refers to the up and down characteristic of the market; also the excitement and drama of the market. Used often in such expressions as "tape action" and "market action."

Advice   Euphemism used to denote the process where brokers make market decisions for their customers.

Advance/decline ratios   Technical term used to compare the number of stocks that have advanced in price as compared to those that have declined in price. A widely used technical indicator.

American Stock Exchange   The second of the two, older, major stock exchanges that are located in New York. Generally is the exchange in which smaller companies are traded. Recently merged with NASD.

Analyst   A person whose primary job is to research and evaluate companies. Some analysts also maintain a few of their own accounts, but most work strictly on a salary basis and do not have any direct sales responsibilities.

Arbitrage   A trading strategy to take advantage of a price difference between two or more linked financial instruments by buying one and selling the other at the same time.

Ask; Asking price   See *bid/ask*.

Auction; Auction market   In general, a market system in which buyers compete with each other by offering "better/higher" prices for an object. In various financial markets, sellers also compete with each other at the same time by offering "better/lower" prices.

Back office   Refers to that segment of a firm that has little or no direct relationship with the public but is responsible for nearly all "housekeeping" chores.

Bears   Name applied to those people who tend to have a negative view of the market, in other words, they think the market is likely to go down. All individuals can be "bearish" at times, but there are some who are perennially so.

Bear trap   Expression used to describe temporary market decline that stimulates selling or shorting, followed by a significant advance in the market.

Bell   Refers to the bell that is sounded to open and close trading on the New York Stock Exchange.

Beta   Technical term for the volatility of a stock. Stocks that fluctuate a great deal will have a high beta and will be considered high-risk stocks. A beta equal to one means the volatility is equal to that of the market as a whole.

Bid/ask   Denotes the current price someone is willing to pay for a particular stock (the bid) and the price someone is willing to sell the stock for (the ask). Under normal conditions, the bid/ask will fractionally bracket the last transaction—so if the last sale was at 25, the bid/ask is likely to be 24⅞ to 25⅛. In an advancing market, however, it may jump to 25¼ to 25½. Similarly, in a declining market it may drop to 24⅞ to 24½. See *quote*.

Big Board   Term used to refer to the New York Stock Exchange.

Blocks   Used to refer to large transactions—those usually involving more than ten thousand shares of stocks at a time.

Block houses   Label given to firms that specialize in trading large blocks, usually for institutional investors.

Blue chip Label given to those companies that are well capitalized, have a proven record of earnings, and pay a reasonable dividend.

Bond A financial instrument that entitles someone to a fixed rate of return for a specific amount of money lent for a specific period of time. A bond does not carry with it any sense of ownership.

Book value Phrase generally used to refer to the net value per share of common stock, which is determined by subtracting all debts and priority claims from the net assets carried on the balance sheet of the company and dividing that by the number of common shares.

Bottom Term used to denote the lows set by the market. Technicians often like to talk about double and triple bottoms, which signify that the market has held at a certain point two or three times. See *support level.*

Boxing See *selling against the box.*

Breakout A term used usually by technicians to indicate that a stock has moved into a new, higher trading range.

Broker Label given to those employed by market firms whose primary duty is to sell stocks and otherwise to service accounts.

Bull Opposite of bear. Person who believes that the market is going up. A bullish attitude is one that reflects such a view of the market.

Buying down Buying program in which additional stock is bought after original purchase if and as the stock declines. The purpose is to lower the average cost paid for the stock. This approach is normally limited to stocks that one expects to hold for a considerable length of time.

Buy order What it says: an order to buy a stock. See *market order* and *limit order.*

CD Certificate of Deposit. Basically an unsecured note of a bank, issued for a limited period of time at a rate slightly under the prime rate, historically in denominations of $100,000, with many banks now offering their own CDs at lower denominations; $100,000, plus CDs are now often referred to as jumbo CDs.

Call The right to buy a stock at a predetermined price. See *option* and *put.* Such rights are sold as if they were stocks.

Capital Term used to refer to moneys used for investment purposes as well as moneys already invested in a corporate structure.

Capital gain/loss Profit or loss resulting from sale of some security or other capital asset. See *long-term profits/losses* and *short-term profits/losses.*

Cash account An account in which all transactions must be settled in full on a cash basis within a specific period of days, normally five working days.

Cash equivalencies   Used to refer to financial instruments such as Treasury Bills and corporate paper, usually with brief duration, which are treated as if they were cash.

CBOE   Chicago Board Option Exchange. The first, and still major, option exchange.

Chartist   Name given to person who follows charts. Only a few so-called Chartists are, in fact, True Believers in the Cyclist-Chartist credo. Most so-called Chartists simply use charts as their main selling tool.

Charts   There are numerous different types of charts. In all cases, however, they graphically record various aspects of past market activity, such as price and volume, in an effort to discover market patterns.

Churn   Name given to process whereby a broker constantly buys and sells stocks for an account, thereby generating commissions for himself.

Closed-end fund   Name given to a type of investment fund that issues a specific number of shares and that can be bought into only by purchasing such shares. See *open-end fund.*

Commercial paper   Similar to Certificate of Deposit, except that it is issued by corporations.

Commission   The fee charged by a brokerage firm for buying or selling stocks. At full-service brokerage houses, this fee ranges between 1 and 1½ percent of the sums involved. Of this sum, the broker keeps between 25 and 40 percent, with the rest going to the firm. At various discount houses, the fee may be as low as a few pennies a share. See also *negotiated commissions.*

Contrarian   A person who tends to act in opposition to the dominant mood of the market. Many market professionals like to think of themselves as contrarians, but few in fact are.

Convertibles   Refers to a range of securities, usually bonds, that are convertible to common stock at a set price normally 10–15 percent above the market price of the stock when the bond is issued. Normally, convertibles are offered at an interest rate below the going rate, since the owner has an opportunity for capital gains if the stock of the company appreciates in value sufficiently to make the convertible options worthwhile.

Correction   Term used to explain decline in market that is considered to be an upward move. It is a Wall Street aphorism that the market never goes straight up or straight down. See *technical rally.*

Cover to cover   Name for process whereby a person buys a stock or an option that they previously sold without owning it. When the stock was originally sold, it was "borrowed." To complete the transaction, it now needs to be bought in the open market and returned to the party who had lent it. See *short.*

Crash   Sudden and large market decline.

Curb, The   The informal, now somewhat archaic, name for the American Stock Exchange that originally did business on the street in front of the New York Stock Exchange.

Cycles   Used most often by Cyclist-Chartists to indicate the rhythmic character of the market.

Cyclicals   Refers to the stocks of such basic industries as steel and chemicals that tend to move in tandem with economic cycles.

Day order   A buy or sell order that expires if not executed on the day it is entered.

Diamonds/DJIA diamonds   Basket of stocks constructed to reflect the Dow Jones Industrial Index; traded as a single equity on the American Stock Exchange. See also *SPDR.*

Discount house   Firm that charges lower commissions for executing market transactions than the pre-May 1975 minimum set rates of the New York Stock Exchange. See *negotiated commissions.*

Discretionary account   An account where the broker has been given a limited power of attorney to manage the account.

Distribution   Term used to signify that a large sophisticated investor is selling stock to less sophisticated small investors. Normally considered a bearish sign for a stock. Opposite of *accumulation.*

Diversification   Practice of investing monies in a number of different stocks as a form of protection in case one stock does very badly.

Dividend   The amount of money that is paid pro rata to the owners of shares of a company. This money, which generally comes from the earnings of the company, is likely to vary with the fortunes of the company.

Dow, the Dow   A major stock market index based upon thirty actively traded blue-chip stocks. More accurately, it is the "Dow Industrial Index." There is also a Transportation Index and a Utility Index, based respectively upon a number of leading transportation stocks and utility stocks. Also referred to colloquially as Dow Jones Averages.

Down and out   An expression used to describe a specific type of "limited risk" call option, traded by only a limited number of Wall Street firms. It usually entails a variable premium for a period of six months, with the striking price approximately the current market price. If, however, the stock declines 10 percent, the option becomes void regardless of the subsequent action of the underlying stock. There is also a refund clause if the option is exercised within the first five months. See *option* and *up and away*.

Downtick   A transaction that occurs at a lower price than the previous transaction of the stock in question.

Earnings   The amount of money earned by a particular company. Earnings are generally stated as per share earnings, i.e., the amount of money earned by the company for each share.

ECN   Electronic Communication Network; used to match trades, primarily of NASDAQ listed stocks, electronically. See *Instinet*.

Economy   General term used to cover the combined activities of all institutions involved in the economic life of a particular political unit be it a city, state, country, geographical area, or the world.

Efficient Market theory   Theory that states that the market responds to all information so efficiently that the price of stocks at any time reflects their true value at that time.

Exchange   Refers to the New York Stock Exchange. May also be used to refer to the American Exchange or any of the various regional exchanges; Chicago, Pacific, Philadelphia, Boston, or Midwest Exchanges. All but the Boston Exchange are engaged in option trading. Could also include the NASDAQ market.

Exercise price, exercise   The same as striking price. The price established for buying or selling the underlying stock for a particular option. To *exercise* entails buying or selling as stipulated by the contract.

Fed   Term used to refer to the Federal Reserve Bank, which controls interest rates and the amount of money in circulation.

Firm; the firm   Colloquial label used to refer to a brokerage institution; used interchangeably with "House." As an unrelated adjective, the term "firm" means that a bid won't disappear, in the immediate future.

Floor broker   A member of the exchange who actually trades on the floor of the exchange. It can refer to persons: trading for their firms and/or the public customers of the firm; trading for themselves (though there are fewer of this type now than in the past); or executing trades for other firms (this group has historically been called "two dollar brokers"). See also *specialist*.

Fourth market   See *third market*.

Fundamentals   Refers to basic economic factors pertaining to a company or the economy in general, such as earnings, dividends, capitalization, debt.

Funds   Name given to any of a range of institutions that invest other people's money. Individuals or institutions give their money to such funds and allow the funds to invest the money as the funds see fit.

Futures   A contract to take delivery of some product at a future date at a specified price.

Gap   Term used to describe situation where a stock opens at a price significantly different from its closing price.

Glamour stocks   Name given to any of a number of stocks that have a record of growing earnings, often a high degree of sophisticated technology, high volatility, and that usually trade at a high multiple of earnings.

Good buying   Buying that originates with persons or institutions that have a reputation for being right more often than wrong. Often it is not so much that they are right as it is that they have a lot of money to invest.

Growth   The term used to indicate that a company is expanding and can consequently be expected to have higher earnings in the future.

Head and shoulders   Chartist's expression used to describe a specific trading pattern that graphically gives the appearance of a frontal view of a person's head and shoulders. Such patterns are seen as indicating a coming market decline.

Heavy   Term used to describe the market or a stock when it fails to rally as briskly as would be liked.

Hedge fund   A fund that is allowed to sell stocks short and operate in other ways prohibited to most public funds.

Hedging   A process whereby one buys or sells a financial instrument, normally an option or a future, as a protective measure to counterbalance another investment. If one owns a stock, for example, one can hedge by buying a put with an exercise price below the present price of the stock.

Held, not held   Terms used to denote two types of "market orders." A not-held order allows the floor broker more discretion in determining the timing in executing an order than does a held order, which must be executed immediately without price restrictions. See *market order* and *limit order.*

Highs, new highs   Terms for stocks trading either in an all-time high or a new high for the year (usually the latter).

Income   Usually refers to dividends that a stock pays or the interest that a bond pays, in contrast to moneys made through capital gains.

Index   Refers to any of the more common "averages" used to measure stock prices, such as the S&P (Standard and Poor's) Index, the New York Stock Exchange Index, the Dow Jones Index, or the Russell 2000 or 3000.

Index fund   A fund that attempts to duplicate the major market indexes such as the Dow or the Standard and Poor's. Most such funds are governed by some variation of the Efficient Market theory of the stock market.

In the money   Another phrase used in connection with options to indicate that the underlying stock is selling at a price above the exercise price of a call option and under the exercise price of a put option. See *out of the money*.

Instinet   An ECN managed by Reuters for electronically matching NASDAQ trades. Systems such as this are now estimated to carry 25 percent of all NASDAQ trades.

Institution   Term used to refer to mutual funds, bank trust departments, and other large fund groups. Used to distinguish large, professional investors from individual investors.

Institutional broker   Adjective used commonly on Wall Street supposedly to separate those who deal with lay investors from those who deal with funds, trust departments, organizations. In fact, used more to locate someone in the class structure of the market than to define actual function.

Investor   Someone who buys stocks for income and long-term growth, as opposed to a quick capital gain (speculator). Also term used by speculators to define themselves when they have bought a stock that hasn't worked out.

IPO, initial public offering   The first public stock offering of a corporation. See *underwriting*.

IRA, individual retirement account   An account that allows individuals to invest pretax dollars, normally up to $2,000 per year, in a retirement investment fund.

Keogh plan   Name given to individual investment retirement programs subject to various tax advantages.

Leaps   Options with more than a year's expiration time.

Lettered stock   Restricted stock of a company that are held normally by company owners and cannot be freely traded. Such stocks generally have the same value as the traded stock, but since they cannot be traded, often sell at a discount.

Lift   An upward movement in the market after a decline. The term *lift* is used more often to signify an interday upward movement. See also *technical rally/decline*.

Limit order   A buy or sell order that is placed with a specific price attached to it. For example, a sell order at 45 means that it cannot be sold for less than 45.

Listed stock   Stock that is registered with and traded on one of the major exchanges—usually either the New York Stock Exchange NASDAQ or the American Stock Exchange.

Liquidity (1) When used in reference to a specific company, refers to the cash flow of the company in relation to its cash needs. A company may have sufficient assets to cover liabilities but still have a cash-flow, i.e., liquidity, problem. (2) When used in reference to the market itself, refers to the volume of trading characteristic of a stock. A stock that trades in low volume is considered to have low liquidity. Fundamentalists are more interested in the first type of liquidity, traders in the second.

Load, no-load Terms used to distinguish between different types of mutual funds. The load type entails an up-front charge when you buy into the fund, whereas a no-load fund does not.

Long-term profits/losses Profits and/or losses incurred on stocks owned for a sufficient period of time (in the past, six months; presently, a year) that allow them to be treated as long-term capital gains or losses for income-tax purposes.

Loss Something that no one on Wall Street likes to talk about.

Margin The amount of money that must be put up in buying a stock. Margin varies with economic and market conditions. In recent years it has fluctuated between 50 and 75 percent, which means that one must put up 50 percent of the value of the stock bought or 75 percent of the value of the stock bought.

Margin call If a stock that one has bought on the margin declines in price, one may receive a margin call, which requires that the owner of the stock to put up more money or be forced to sell the stock.

Market maker A NASD member firm that competes with other firms to make a market in a particular security. Such firms normally participate by maintaining public buy and sell quotations for a guaranteed number of shares in the stock.

Market order An order to buy or sell a stock immediately without price restrictions. See *limit order.*

Momentum A market concept based on the notion that the stock market tends to continue to move in the direction in which it is moving.

Money manager A person who runs portfolios for wealthy individuals or institutions.

Most-active list Exactly what it says: the list of those stocks that have traded in the most volume during a specific period of time.

Move   Either an advance or decline of a stock or the stock market as a whole of some significance.

Multiple   See *P/E*.

Mutual fund   See *funds, closed-end fund, open-end fund.*

Naked option   Refers to an option that is sold without the seller owning the underlying stock.

NASD   The National Association of Securities Dealers, which is the association of brokers and dealers that is responsible for running the NASDAQ and the over-the-counter markets.

NASDAQ   Refers to the integrated market maintained by the various members of NASD and the companies traded in this market. Also used to refer to index of this market, based on values of these companies.

Negotiated commissions   Since May 1, 1975, member firms of the New York Stock Exchange can offer discounts to customers if they so wish. This has given rise to what is now called negotiated commissions.

New York Stock Exchange   The largest stock exchange, located at the intersection of Wall Street and Broad Street in New York City.

New York Stock Exchange Index   An index based upon all of the stocks traded on the New York Stock Exchange. One of the most broad-based indexes used.

Nifty-fifty   Somewhat archaic label that was given to the fifty major companies that were the current favorites of institutional investors. Most of these companies were very large corporate institutions, but they also included a relatively high number of high multiple glamour stocks.

No-load fund   A mutual fund that can be bought directly from the investment company and that is sold without any up-front sales commission.

Odd lot, odd lotter   Name given to trades and individuals who trade in less than one hundred share units. The odd lotter is often used as a contrary index by technicians—when the odd lotter is buying, the market is going to go down, and vice versa.

Open-end fund   A fund, generally a mutual fund, that is constantly attempting to raise more capital. It is considered an open-ended fund since there is no limit on the amount of money that can be invested through the fund. See *closed-end fund.*

Option   The right to either buy or sell a stock at a fixed price for a specific period of time.

Out of the money   Phrase used to denote an option whose underlying stock is trading under the options exercise price, in the case of a call, or above its exercise price, in the case of a put option.

Over the Counter (OTC)   Stocks are sold and bought through dealer brokers rather than through specialists. Most smaller companies trade in the OTC market since the capitalization requirements are much less than those of the major exchanges. In recent years, with the growth of the NASDAQ market, many large companies have elected to stay with this market. See *NASD* and *NASDAQ*.

Paper   See *commercial paper*.

Portfolio   Refers to the actual holdings—such as stocks, bonds, T-bills—in a given account.

Preferred stock   A class of stock with priority rights over common stock in securing its dividend, which is normally specified. Preferred stocks normally also have priority rights over common stock of the same company to assets in case of liquidation of the company.

Premium   Refers to value in excess of the face value of a bond and/or the value in excess of the exercise price of an option.

P/E, price/earnings   The ratio of the price of a stock divided by the annual per share earnings of the company. Most people consider a P/E between 8 and 12 as fairly standard, with a lower or higher P/E indicating either expectations of dramatically higher earnings or lower earnings in the future.

Prime, prime rate   The interest rate set by banks for their best customers.

Public   Used to refer to all those who are not professionally involved in the market. More recently the "public" is often contrasted with "institutional" participants.

Put   An option to sell a stock at a set price for a specified period of time.

Quality   Adjective generally applied to companies and their stock that are seen to have superior management, a record of good earnings, and a record of consistent dividend payments.

Quote   Term used to denote the present price of a stock, normally coupled with the bid/ask prices.

Rally   A fairly rapid upward movement in the market, more often than not following a significant decline.

Random walk   Phrase used most by Efficient Market theorists to indicate that there is no discernible pattern to a series of events, such as stock prices. The implication is that it is a purely random affair whether a stock will go up or down at any moment.

RR, registered representative   The official New York Stock Exchange term for brokers.

Research department   What every brokerage house claims to have.

Resistance area   Phrase referring to price level where the market as a whole or a specific stock has in the past run into heavy selling pressure, which has prevented the stock or the market as a whole to move higher in price. See *support level.*

Return, rate of return   Term used to refer to total gains including capital appreciation and dividends or yield from an investment.

Rights   See *warrants.*

Roth IRA   Relatively new type of IRA in which the money invested is after-tax funds, but where all future gains are tax free. Subject to various income limitations.

Seat   Term used to refer to membership in a given exchange, for example, "a seat on the New York Stock Exchange."

SEC   The Securities Exchange Commission. The federal government regulatory agency, established in the early thirties, responsible for overseeing the market.

Secondary market   Expression used to refer to resale of securities after their initial offering (see *IPO*). In effect refers to majority of all security transactions. See also *third market.*

Selling against the box   A process whereby someone sells short a stock that he or she owns using that stock as collateral. For tax reasons, however, the brokerage firm executing such an order must either use its own stock or borrow stock to sell, creating thereby two separate transactions. A widely used technique to avoid incurring a tax liability within a given fiscal year.

Service   (1) Term used to refer to the numerous brokerage functions that are not directly related to executing orders, such as supplying recommendations, checking out a specific company, evaluating a portfolio. (2) Referring to any of a number of market advisory services ranging from the Value Line letter to any of the here-today, gone-tomorrow market letters.

Short   To sell a stock that one does not own in the anticipation that it will go lower and allow one to buy it back for less money than one sold it at. To sell short, one must be able to borrow the stock. One will usually borrow from the brokerage house with which one does business. See also *selling against the box* for another variation of this procedure.

Short interest   Indicator that reveals the number of shares that have been sold short in a particular company and the market as a whole. Many consider a large short interest to be bullish—it indicates that there is a large demand for stocks, since every short seller has sold a stock without owning it.

Short-term profits/losses   Refers to capital gains or losses that result from sale of stock held for a period of less than a year. Such profits and losses are treated like unearned income for tax purposes.

Shot to take a shot   Expression used to indicate a more speculative investment.

Sideways market   A market that can't make up its mind whether it wants to go up or down.

Small investor   Generally considered to be any investor with annual income of less than $25,000 and a portfolio of under $10,000.

Source   Refers to persons who are considered to have "inside" or other "good" information. Nearly every professional in the market relies to some extent upon a source or two.

SPDR/Spider (S&P Depository Receipts)   Basket of stocks constructed to reflect the Standard and Poor's (S&P) Index, traded as a single equity on the American Stock Exchange. See also *diamonds.*

Specialist   A member of the exchange who is given the responsibility by the exchange to make a market in a particular stock.

Specialist's book   The book a specialist keeps that records the various buy and sell orders that he has been given at prices either above or below the market. See *limit order.*

Speculator   Term used to distinguish those people who buy stocks primarily for capital gains rather than for income. Speculators are usually interested in short-term gains.

Split   When a stock is divided into any number of shares to adjust its price to a range that is considered preferable for future sales. A stock that has gone from 20 to 40 may be split two-for-one to bring its price back to 20. Sometimes there are reverse splits where a stock that has gone from 5 to 1 may be reissued at a 5 for 1 ratio to bring it back to 5. There are many different types of splits: 3 for 2, 5 for 4, and so on.

Spread   Can refer to the difference between the bid and ask price of a stock or to any of a number of differences in price between various options associated with a given stock.

Squeeze, short squeeze   Describes situation where an upward movement in the price of a stock puts pressure upon those who have sold the stock short. Short sellers may then be forced to cover their position, forcing the stock up further and thus repeating the process for those who have shorted the stock at a higher price.

Stop-buy order   A trading technique—less used than stop-loss orders—in which a stock is automatically purchased if the stock trades at a specific price above or below the market.

Stop/loss order   A popular trading technique among traders. A specific price below the current market for a stock (a price that the trader feels for any of a number of reasons should not be penetrated by the stock) at which the stock is to be automatically sold.

Story   Information that is more than a tip but less than confirmed; to some, the lifeblood of the market.

Straddle   Refers to the trading strategy of buying or selling an equivalent number of puts or calls on a given underlying stock with the same exercise price and expiration date.

Street account   Phrase used to denote customer accounts in which stocks are kept in the firm name rather than formally transferred to customers. Common in accounts whose stocks are bought on margin. Many customers also prefer such accounts because the brokerage firm maintains and provides monthly records of all transactions and holdings.

Striking price   See *exercise price.*

Superdot   An electronic ordering system used by the New York Stock Exchange for direct matching of market and limit orders by member firms. See *Instinet* and *ECN.*

Support level   Expression used to indicate that at a certain price below the present price of a stock or the market as a whole, there exist significant buy orders that will not allow the stock to drop below that price. Though the concept of support levels is associated most often with Cyclist-Chartists, most market participants "believe" in a variety of support levels.

Symbol   The letter combinations that are used to denote a company on the tape.

Takeover   Phrase used to describe process whereby one company takes control of another company, usually by making a special offering to buy the outstanding stock of the "taken over" company.

Tape   The ongoing and generally up-to-the-minute record of all stock transactions. At one time it truly was a tape, with each exchange publishing its own tape. Today, it is more likely to be an electronic board that combines the transactions of all exchanges. Sometimes also used to refer to the ongoing "publication" of the various news services, such as Dow Jones and Reuters.

Tax selling Expression used to categorize selling that is seen to be due to a desire to take losses in a given taxable year to offset gains. December is a month in which there is usually a good deal of tax selling.

Technical rally/decline A rally in what is generally considered to be a down market, or a decline in an up market, that is due not so much to a change in the market but rather to the fact that the market never goes straight down or up.

Ten-K/10-K Refers to the detailed financial form that must be filed with the Security and Exchange Commission. Many persons consider these forms to be much more accurate statements of a company's financial position than its annual reports.

Text The market is said to be "testing" previous lows or highs when it approaches in price these previous lows or highs. See *support level.*

Third market Expression used to refer to those transactions involving listed stocks between large institutional houses that do not go through the exchange, but are rather direct transactions between the buying and selling parties. Such transactions are normally executed through a NASD firm. When there is no NASD firm participation, such transactions are often referred to as constituting a fourth market.

Ticker See *tape.*

Top Term used to denote the high prices set by the market. As with the concept of market bottom, technicians often refer to double and triple tops. See *resistance area.*

Trader A market participant who moves in and out of the market often and with speed. See chapter 5.

Trading room Term used to refer to that segment of a firm where orders are usually executed. A salesman will forward his order to his trading room, which will in turn forward the order to the floor of the exchange—to their person on the floor. It is the responsibility of the trading room to get the best possible execution for any order; to do this, it must keep in constant touch with what is going on within the exchanges themselves.

Transaction A market trade.

Triple witching hour The last trading hour on the third Friday of March, June, September, and December, when options and futures on stock indexes expire concurrently.

Two dollar broker A floor broker who will trade for another brokerage house for a set commission (historically two dollars) per hundred shares. Many smaller brokerage houses with a limited number of floor brokers make use of such persons. See *floor broker.*

Underwriting   Process in which investment banks bring new stock offerings to the market. Such banks, either individually or in small groups, normally purchase the stock to be sold from the company at a fixed price and then attempt to resell it in the public market.

Unlisted stock   A publicly held company that is not listed and, therefore, not traded on an existing exchange. Often used to refer, however, to stocks that are only listed and traded in the Over the Counter market.

Up and away   The put counterpart to a *down and out.* A "limited risk put option" sold normally for a six-month period at a variable premium and that becomes void if the underlying stock appreciates by 10 percent or more.

Volatility   Refers to the degree to which a stock moves up and down relative to its price. A stock that tends to go up and down regularly is considered to be a highly volatile stock, whereas one that does not is considered to be nonvolatile. See also *beta.*

Volume   Refers to the number of shares traded in a given period of time.

Warrants   Rights to buy a stock at a certain price. Warrants are issued by the company itself to present stockholders, often in lieu of dividends. In many ways they are like a call option, but they are rights to company-held stock rather than to stock already being traded.

Window dressing   Refers to a fairly common practice of institutional funds whereby the fund sells and buys stocks near the end of a quarter in order to improve the appearance of the portfolio. The fund will sell a stock that has performed poorly, thereby not having to show that they owned it, and will buy stocks that have done well, giving the impression that they were very astute. In actuality, such window dressing cannot only not make money but also can cost money; many fund managers, however, feel that it helps sales of the fund.

Whiplash, whipsaw   Terms used to refer to a situation in which a stock moves in one direction and then suddenly moves strongly in the other direction. Common among highly volatile stocks. This term is usually only used for situations where one has bought the stock in an upward movement only to see it then go down, or has shorted the stock in the downward movement only to see it then go up.

Wrap/wrapped account   An account with a set management fee—usually 1 to 2 percent of the value of the account where the management fee covers all commissions and other normal brokerage charges.

Yield   Dividend or interest paid on a security.

NOTES

1. Robert K. Merton (1987), "Three Fragments from a Sociologist's Note-books: Establishing the Phenomenon, Specified Ignorance and Strategic Research Materials," *Annual Review of Sociology*, vol. 13, pp. 1–28.
2. There is a good deal of competition between the NYSE and NASDAQ, and each likes to claim it is bigger. Recently the NASDAQ has often claimed more volume than the NYSE, but it should be noted that whereas buys and sells are recorded individually on the NASDAQ they are recorded as a single transaction on the NYSE.
3. Twenty years ago, all of the professionals in my book were male. In this book we will meet a number of females, reflecting the changing gender demographics of Wall Street.
4. See "Glossary" for definition of market terms used in text.
5. That the stock market should be clothed in ambiguity is not that surprising, given that it remains primarily an auction market. Auction markets by their very nature are both the product of and producers of ambiguity. For a more detailed discussion of the relationship between auction markets in general and ambiguity, see my book *Auctions: The Social Construction of Value* (New York: Free Press, 1989; paperback edition, Berkeley and Los Angeles: University of California Press, 1990.)
6. Although the comments presented tend to be more cynical than the comments one would likely get from a similar group of market professionals today, I would argue that they still accurately reflect a general recognition of the fickleness of the market.
7. This statement is somewhat dated, but not completely. As we will see, more and more market professionals are using index and quasi-index funds. Most, however, continue to share Jack Reed's concern that by doing so they are managing themselves out of their own jobs.

8. It should be stressed that when Ben Decker made this statement, he was talking about people trying to outperform the market in general and other forms of investment. Given the overall performance of the market in recent years, I am quite confident that Ben would favor allocating a significant sum of money into well-managed index funds, but he wouldn't really consider this being in the market in the sense implied in the text.

9. As we will see, this remains a real problem. The idea of Wrap accounts, which will be discussed in part 3, represents a more recent strategy for dealing with this issue.

10. One of the big changes in the market over the last decade or so has been redefining what it means to beat the market. Twenty years ago, beating the market meant obtaining a better return on your money than you could get elsewhere—bonds, real estate, or others. Today, it merely means doing better than the major indexes. This is an issue to which we will return.

11. The issue of intentionality of knowledge has been discussed and analyzed by many. I would recommend my own *A Critique of Sociological Reasoning* (Oxford: Basil Blackwell Publishers; and Totowa, N.J.: Rowman & Littlefield, 1979); Karl Mannheim's *Ideology and Utopia*, Pt. 1 (New York: Harvest Books, 1936); Peter Berger and Thomas Luckmann, *The Social Construction of Reality* (Garden City, New York: Anchor Books, 1967); and Anthony Giddens, *The Constitution of Society* (Berkeley: University of California Press, 1984). That there are different types of interests is a related but analytically distinct question. In addition to the works just cited, see Jurgen Habermas, *Knowledge and Human Interest* (Boston: Beacon Press, 1971).

12. The euphemism of "juggling the books" covers a wide range of behavior from outright fraud to the more familiar practice of treating various earnings and costs in a somewhat questionable manner. One example of this is reporting higher earnings and then noting a special, one-time write-off of some loss rather than adjusting one's earnings to account for this loss.

13. There is, of course, nothing peculiar about the market in this respect. All meanings are social by definition and are based upon some sort of consensus. This issue is discussed at length in the Mannheim (1936), Berger and Luckmann (1967), and Smith (1979). Such knowledge also need not be conscious. See Giddens (1987).

14. Figures drawn from the *Fact Book for the Year 1997* published by the New York Stock Exchange in 1998.

15. This is one of the key classical insights of sociology that has been made in different ways by different theorists. More recently well formulated by

Giddens as ontological insecurity. It was key to my understanding of the market twenty years ago and is true today.

16. See Berger and Luckmann, *Social Construction,* pp. 117ff.

17. My use of the term "True Believer" is meant to imply an intellectual position, but one that serves also as the grounds for action.

18. Twenty years ago, I deliberately referred to four spokesmen rather than to spokespersons. In doing so, I accurately reflected the overwhelming male dominance of the market. Women are still under-represented among market professionals, especially in light of their ownership role. They are nevertheless better represented today than twenty years ago, which is reflected in the appearance here of a mixed gender group.

19. In most cases, such anonymity was guaranteed.

20. Although most of the descriptions presented are based on interactions that occurred some years ago, they remain accurate descriptions of the group that Bill Chester represents.

21. It is difficult to make broad generalizations regarding preferences for general economic news versus financial news when discussing true Fundamentalists. My experience indicates, however, that although most who claim to be Fundamentalists indicate a preference for strictly financial news, most true Fundamentalists are more concerned with general economic news.

22. Bill Chester's selling tended to be more intensive because he accumulated stock over a period of time. When he felt his stocks were fully valued, however, he wanted to get out as quickly as possible.

23. This view is reflected perfectly in Warren Buffett's recently quoted comment that he wouldn't and couldn't buy the high-growth technology stocks like Microsoft and Cisco because he didn't understand such companies.

24. It is difficult to generalize about institutional salesmen, because their role varies from firm to firm. In general, the larger the firm—the more analysts, the more block traders, the more everything—the more peripheral the institutional salesman is to the actual buying and selling of stocks. In smaller operations, the salesman may actually be involved in the execution of market orders.

25. In Hank's heyday, the international money scene played a secondary role. During the last decade it has come to play a major role.

26. Providing female companionship as well as food and drink represented then and now one of the seamier sides of the market. Because most involved in this type of behavior don't like to talk about it, it is difficult to

know how extensive it is. From my experience, I would judge the practice to be no more nor less common than it is in any "sales relationship" in which substantial sums of money are involved and "customer service" plays an important role. To the extent that the stock market is today less a male preserve, I would guess that such practices are less common.

27. For an excellent review of the way in which self regulation has grown in the market and its overall effect on trading, see Mitchell Abolafia's *Making Markets* (Cambridge: Harvard University Press, 1996).

28. An option to buy a stock trading at $98 at $100 for one month might, for example, be bought for $2. In effect this means that one is being asked to pay a $4 premium—$2 for the option plus $2 for the difference between the present price of $98 and the right to buy it for $100—for the right to buy the stock within the month. On the other hand, one is only risking the $2 option price, not the $98 it would have cost to buy the stock. Moreover, if the stock goes to $120, one will make ten times one's investment ($20 for $2), yet the person owning the stock will only make approximately 20 percent ($22 on $98).

29. As Abolafia notes in *Making Markets,* future and option markets entail less self-regulation than do the major stock markets. It should be noted, however, that the resulting volume increases in option and future sales are often more easily detected than corresponding increases in the volume of the underlying stock.

30. The term "insider" is used here, as it is used on the street, to refer to company executives and large stockholders who are required to report their own transactions in their company, not the Insider prototype that is the focus of this chapter.

31. In presenting a spokesperson for the Cyclist-Chartist perspective, I not only have changed the gender of the spokesperson but also have switched the time frame to the present. The gender switch reflects not only the greater participation of women on Wall Street but also the fact that among the actual people used in constructing this prototype there were a number of women. I also elected to switch the time frame, even though many of the comments were made some years ago, because most are as appropriate to this view today as they were previously. This was not the case with Bill Chester and Hank Strong, many of whose comments pertained to the time they were made.

32. It is this belief in an underlying order to the market that separates Ann Klein and other true Cyclist-Chartists from those who simply make use of

technical information. This point will be developed in more detail in analyzing the technically oriented salesmen of the market.

33. Ann Klein is fairly extreme in this regard even for a Cyclist-Chartist. Many
people who qualify as true Cyclist-Chartists favor a more probabilistic view
toward their charts and consequently are more willing to admit that their
charts may be wrong at times.

34. Though Ann Klein is highly sensitive to what is called "price momentum,"
she is not in the strict sense of the term a price-momentum investor. True
price-momentum investors aren't concerned about long-term patterns but
rather with the specific price momentum of the moment that they seek to
ride. In this respect, most momentum players have more in common with
Traders, who are discussed in chapter 5.

35. If John Holland has a "market bible," it is G. M. Loeb's *The Battle for
Investment Survival* (New York: Simon & Schuster, 1957).

36. Or, more accurately, "Buy low, sell when fairly valued."

37. For a discussion of how things have changed on the floor of the New York
Stock Exchange and for the floor specialist, see Abolafia, *Making Markets*,
chapters 5 and 6.

38. For what has become perhaps the classic argument for, as well as a level-
headed, nontechnical treatment of, the Efficient Market theory, plus for
an extensive bibliography, see Burton G. Malkiel, *A Random Walk Down
Wall Street* (New York: Norton, 1973). There have been a number of re-
vised editions since 1973.

39. Though the great majority of all registered reps are still paid on a commis-
sion-plus basis, there is evidence of some significant changes in this system.
At the low end, more and more brokers working for discount houses are
paid a flat salary until, at least, they become significant producers. At the
high end of the business, many brokers are attempting to move more and
more accounts into what is called a wrap account. Such accounts earn an
overall management fee—usually between 2 and 2.5 percent—which covers transaction fees. In a good number of these cases, the funds are then
invested in the equivalent of a mutual fund, either the brokerage house's
own or a public fund, and the registered rep serves more as a general
financial adviser making basic allocation decisions.

40. See the New York Stock Exchange *Fact Book for the Year 1997*, pp. 77–78.
It is difficult to generalize from these figures to all firms, because not all
firms are equally involved in underwriting and firm trading, i.e., trading
firm money. In some firms, these activities may each account for 25 per-

cent of the firm's gross earnings, yet in other firms they may account for practically nothing. Percentages vary from year to year.

41. For an interesting, if somewhat biased, view of this issue see *The Registered Representative*: A Look above the Bottom Line (New York Stock Exchange, 1975).

42. A summary of the rules can be obtained from the Securities and Exchange Commission (SEC), as well as from the various exchanges and a number of brokerage houses.

43. See *The Registered Representative*.

44. Although, as noted earlier, the number of female registered representatives has increased significantly, men still outnumber the women by better than three to one. Consequently, though I often refer to this group throughout this book as salespersons, I have taken the liberty in this section to refer to them as salesmen.

45. Twenty years ago, I presented the Market Salesman as a pseudo-Cyclist-Chartist due to the fact that the Efficient Market view was not fully articulated.

46. There is a significant amount of feedback in this situation. Both Customer Salesmen and Action Salesmen, as well as Traders, tend to favor the stocks that move a lot, since they account for a good deal of market action.

47. For the record, I should probably note that there has been a great deal of truth to this view during the last decade. How true it will remain over a longer period of time is quite another matter that only the future will reveal.

48. For a brief, but quite inclusive review of such "mass behavior" see my *Critique*, pp. 62–67. For some classical formulations see Gustave LeBon, *The Crowd* (London: T. F. Unwin, 1921); Sigmund Freud, *Group Psychology and the Analysis of the Ego* (New York: Bantam, 1960); Ralph H. Turner and Lewis M. Killian, *Collective Behavior* (Englewood Cliffs, N.J.: Prentice-Hall, 1957); and Stanley Milgram and Hans Toch, "Collective Behavior: Crowds and Social Movements," in *The Handbook of Social Psychology*, ed. Gardner Lindzey and Elliot Aronson (Reading, Mass.: Addison-Wesley, 1968), vol. 4, pp. 507–610.

49. For a more detailed discussion of this process, see Smith, *Critique*, pp. 62–67.

50. The fact that True Believers are less susceptible to the pull of the crowd explains more than anything else why they tend to do better in the market than others do. The real strength of a True Believer is not his or her particular view of the market but rather the commitment to a particular view of

the market. It is not that they are always, or even usually, right, but that they manage to avoid being disastrously wrong. This has important implications for the small investor, who doesn't have to be a genius, only to avoid being a fool. The general implications of this study for the small investor will be reviewed in part 6, "Some Practical Advice for the Individual Investor."

51. In 1987, the Dow Jones Industrial Average (DJIA) rose or fell over 1 percent for 38.3 percent of trading days, compared to 22.1 percent of trading days the previous year and an average of 22.5 percent of trading days for the previous six years. In the six years following 1987, the DJIA rose or fell on only 21 percent of all trading days. DJIA average daily price swings reflect a similar difference in volatility, with 1987 showing a 1.17 percent absolute daily swing, and the previous six years an average swing of .68 percent and the six following years a swing of .63 percent. This represents approximately a 70 percent spurt in volatility. (Data provided by the New York Stock Exchange Website.)

52. The general principles are fairly straightforward, but working out the details is quite complex. So complex, in fact, that Robert K. Merton and Melvyn Scholes were awarded the Nobel Prize in Economics for working out these details.

53. The rule governing this process on the New York Stock Exchange is called Rule 80A. The 2 percent is computed on the closing price of the NYSE Index the preceding quarter.

54. Since its inception, sociology has been fascinated by economic markets. Emile Durkheim, Max Weber, and Georg Simmel—all major early figures in the field—were interested in economic markets. For many years, this interest flagged. More recently, there has been a renewed interest in economic sociology, as evidenced by the publication of the *Handbook of Economic Sociology*, ed. Neil Smelser and Richard Swedberg (Princeton: Princeton University Press; and New York: Russell Sage Foundation, 1994) and numerous other volumes. Most of this interest, however, has taken the form of attempting to show that economic processes could be better understood if they were subject to sociological structural and cultural analysis. Approaching markets from the perspective of the sociology of knowledge has been, for the most part, a much more recent phenomenon.

55. To use Robert K. Merton's notion, the stock market provides an ideal strategic research site for doing work in the social construction of meanings and values. See note 1.

56. What could be called a fourth theme has been the role of experts in defining social reality. The theme was introduced in chapter 1 of this study. What we have discovered, as with so much else, is that expertise varies as objectives change. With the exception of the crowd, however, we have seen that there are always experts of some sort, and even in the case of the crowd there is the assumption that such experts exist.

57. As we saw earlier, Efficient Market enhancers, unlike pure Efficient Market adherents, are also unwilling to surrender completely.

58. The literature on this subject is too great even to list. For a general discussion of the issue, see chapter 7 in my book *Auctions,* and the first part of my *Critique.* Also Habermas, *Knowledge,* and his *Communication and the Evolution of Society* (Boston: Beacon Press, 1979); and Max Weber, *The Theory of Social and Economic Organization,* trans. Talcott Parsons (New York: Free Press, 1947), pp. 88–118. For a more psychologically grounded classical account that wrestles with this issue, look into Piaget. Given his many publications, I would recommend beginning with John H. Flavell's *The Developmental Psychology of Jean Piaget* (Princeton: Von Nostrand, 1963).

59. Although the ordering function of ideas has tended to dominate their generative role, both roles can be found throughout human history. I find it interesting that in my earlier book I only acknowledged their ordering role, but then the market was considerably more ordered at that time. I might note in this context that the tendency to stress the ordering power of ideas over their Transformational power is quite common.

60. Formulated in this way, it may sound as if both Cynics and Faithful are all "closet" Cyclist-Chartists, given that a concern with the underlying order or pattern of the market was earlier shown to be their essential characteristic. The difference is that a Cyclist-Chartist deserving to be called a True Believer is still primarily concerned with mastering the market. Cynics and Faithful want to eliminate ambiguity.

61. More concretely, I noted that a number of Cyclist-Chartists end up as salespersons for discount brokerage firms or sometimes market commentators. In both of these roles, their primary responsibility is to describe in an orderly way what has happened.

62. The first view as indicated in the text is basically that of what generally passes as the scientific, "realist" view. It similarly has much in common with the Weberian concept of means-ends/instrumental rationality. The interpersonal view, meanwhile, has more in common with what may be

called the interpretive/hermeneutic view of rationality. The ideational view has historically been primarily associated with pure philosophy and philosophical theology, though it is also the view of many cognitive psychologists. The last view could be called the classical sociological view insofar as it sees reasoning as inherently normative and as providing the basis for social solidarity. For a more detailed analysis of this issue see Charles W. Smith, "On the Sociology of Mind," in *Explaining Human Behavior*, edited by Paul Secord (Beverly Hills: Sage Publications, 1982).

63. The recent dramatic increase in interest in the stock market raises a number of important questions that, though related to many of the concerns of this book, also transcend them. A preliminary discussion of some of these issues is contained in the "Theoretical and Methodological Note" at the end of the book.

64. This section draws heavily upon a similarly titled appendix included in my *The Mind of the Market.* I am pleased to say that pretty much everything I had to say then holds true today. Changing market conditions, however, have forced me to revise some of the advice I gave earlier regarding the use of the short-loss principle and the use of market orders. Hopefully, the advice offered here will hold up just as well for the next twenty years.

65. I might note that this is a relatively new option, since the number of quality index funds that an investor can choose from today did not exist twenty years ago.

66. The only people I know who can put all of their money in an index fund and leave it there are people who have no real interest in the market. Of course during the last ten years, they have tended to better in the market than anyone else.

67. This situation could result from having picked a stock whose projected value has continued to increase as the stock has appreciated. As such, it might still have the potential for significantly more growth even though it has already gone up considerably. If this stock now represents a larger percentage of your overall portfolio than you believe a single stock should have, however, it may be wise to sell some of it in order to maintain a more balanced, diversified portfolio.

68. See my *Mind of the Market* (Totowa, N.J.: Rowman & Littlefield, 1981); and *Auctions: The Social Construction of Value* (New York: Free Press, 1989; paperback edition, Berkeley and Los Angeles: University of California Press, 1990). This advice applies only to the New York Stock Exchange,

since all stop orders on the American Exchange are automatically stop/limit orders. A stop order at 45 will only be executed at 45.

69. For what is perhaps the classic formulation of the sociology of knowledge see Mannheim, *Ideology and Utopia*. See also Berger and Luckmann, *Social Construction*. For a more recent formulation of the role of knowledge in social life see Giddens, *Constitution of Society*.

70. See my "On the Sociology of Mind" in *Explaining Social Behavior*, ed. Paul F. Secord (Beverly Hills: Sage Publications, 1982).

71. Weber's concern with "rationality" runs throughout his writings. See especially, however, *Theory of Social and Economic Organization*, and *Sociology of Religion* (Boston: Beacon Press, 1963).

72. See the appendix, "Knowledge and Human Interest," in Habermas's *Knowledge and Human Interest*, and his *Legitimation Crisis* (Boston: Beacon Press, 1975).

73. The distinction between tacit and discursive forms of knowledge and the role these different forms play in social life is a theme that runs through nearly all of my research, including this study. For an excellent formulation of this issue, I would recommend Giddens, *Constitution of Society*.

74. The use of prime informers has historically been a major source of sociological data, though such sources are often not explicitly noted. Whole studies have been based upon such sources; see, for example, Edwin H. Sutherland, *The Professional Thief* (Chicago: University of Chicago Press, 1937). More commonly, the prime informer is one source in what is basically a participant observation study; perhaps the classic example of this is William F. Whyte's use of Doc in *Street Corner Society* (Chicago: University of Chicago Press, 1955). Over a period of nearly forty years, I have found such informants to be indispensable in obtaining access and corroborating research findings.

75. By "fairly open," I mean that I never engaged in any form of subterfuge; I quite openly explained that I was interested in understanding how different market participants interpreted and understood the market. I did not, however, as a rule describe the prototypes presented in this book nor any of my more theoretical observations.

76. For a description of similar problems confronted by a person doing a similar type of study, see Michael Maccoby, *The Gamesman* (New York: Simon and Schuster, 1976). Relying, as he did, more upon formal interviews and less upon participant observation, Maccoby was forced to rely more upon persons of influence. For what is perhaps the classic statement on partici-

pant observation, see Whyte, *Street Corner Society*, pp. 299ff. The methodological note in my *Auction* book deals with a number of other issues to this subject. Mitchell Abolafia (1998) reports very similar experiences in his more recent methodological note bearing on his own market research.

77. This growth in interest is evidenced by the growth in publications and organizational activities. To list just a few items: the formation of the *Society for the Advancement of Socio-Economics* (SASE) in the mid-eighties, and the ongoing efforts to organize an Economic Sociology Section in the American Sociological Association. Perhaps more important has been the raft of publications in the area by sociologists over approximately the last decade. To note just some: Neil Smelser and Richard Swedberg, eds., *The Handbook of Economic Sociology* (Princeton: Princeton University Press; and New York: Russell Sage Foundation, 1994); Mark Granovetter and Richard Swedberg, eds., *The Sociology of Economic Life* (Boulder: Westview Press, 1992); Richard Swedberg, ed., *Explorations in Economic Sociology* (New York: Russell Sage Foundation, 1993); Viviana Zelizer, *The Social Meaning of Money* (New York: Basic Books, 1994); Smith, *Auctions;* Amitai Etzioni, *The Moral Dimension* (New York: Free Press, 1988); Swedberg, ed., *Economic and Sociology* (Princeton: Princeton University Press; 1990); Grahame Thompson, Jennifer Frances, Rosalind Levačić, Jeremy Mitchell, *Markets, Hierarchies & Networks* (London: Sage, 1991); Abolafia, *Making Markets* (Cambridge: Harvard University Press, 1996); Mary Zey, *Banking on Fraud* (New York: Aldine, 1993); Roger Friedland and A. F. Robertson, eds., *Beyond the Marketplace* (New York: Aldine, 1990).

78. Twenty years ago, few social scientists outside of economics took market activity very seriously, and among those who did, even fewer approached such markets from a sociology of knowledge perspective. In contrast, practically all professional sociological conferences in recent years have featured at least one or two sessions dealing with these issues.

79. George Soros, *The Crisis of Global Capitalism* (New York: Public Affairs, 1998).

80. See, for example, Soros, *The Crisis of Global Capitalism;* and Anthony Giddens, *The Third Way* (Oxford: Polity Press, 1998).

REFERENCES

Abolafia, Mitchell Y. (1996). *Making Markets: Opportunism and Restraint on Wall Street*. Cambridge, MA: Harvard University Press.

———— (1998). "Markets as Cultures: an ethnographic approach" in The Laws of the Market, Michel Callen, (ed.), Oxford: Basil Blackwell Publisher.

Berger, Peter, and Luckmann, Thomas (1967). *The Social Construction of Reality: A Treatise in the Sociology of Knowledge*. Garden City, NY: Anchor Books.

Etzioni, Amitai (1988). *The Moral Dimension: Toward a New Economics*. New York: Free Press.

Flavell, John H. (1963). *The Developmental Psychology of Jean Piaget.* Princeton, NJ: Von Nostrand.

Freud, Sigmund (1960). *Group Psychology and the Analysis of the Ego*. New York: Bantam Books.

Friedland, Roger, and A. F. Robertson (Eds.) (1990). *Beyond the Marketplace: Rethinking Economy and Society (Sociology and Economics: Controversy and Integration Series)*. New York: Aldine de Gruyter.

Giddens, Anthony (1984). *The Constitution of Society: Outline of the Theory of Structuration*. Berkeley, CA: University of California Press.

———— (1998). *The Third Way: The Renewal of Social Democracy*. Oxford: Polity Press.

Granovetter, Mark S., and Richard Swedberg (Eds.) (1992). *The Sociology of Economic Life*. Boulder: Westview Press.

Habermas, Jurgen (1971). *Knowledge and Human Interest*. Boston: Beacon Press.

———— (1975). *Legitimation Crisis*. Boston: Beacon Press.

———— (1979). *Communication and the Evolution of Society*. Boston: Beacon Press.

LeBon, Gustave (1921). *The Crowd.* London: T. F. Unwin.

Loeb, Gerald M. (1957). *The Battle for Investment Survival.* New York: Simon and Schuster.

Maccoby, Michael (1976). *The Gamesman.* New York: Simon and Schuster.

Malkiel, Burton G. (1973). *A Random Walk Down Wall Street.* New York: Norton.

Mannheim, Karl (1936). *Ideology and Utopia.* New York: Harvest Books.

Mead, George Herbert (1934). *Mind, Self, and Society.* Chicago: University of Chicago Press.

Merton, Robert K. (1987). "Three Fragments from a Sociologist's Notebooks: Establishing the Phenomenon, Specified Ignorance, and Strategic Research Materials," *Annual Review of Sociology,* vol. 13, pp. 1–28.

Milgram, Stanley, and Hans Toch (1954/1969). "Collective Behavior: Crowds and Social Movements" in *The Handbook of Social Psychology,* ed. Gardner Lindzey and Elliot Aronson. Reading, MA: Addison-Wesley. Second Edition, Vol. 4, pp. 507–610.

The New York Stock Exchange (1975). *The Registered Representative: A Look above the Bottom Line.* New York: The New York Stock Exchange, Inc.

——— (1998). *Fact Book for the Year 1997.* New York: The New York Stock Exchange, Inc.

Simmel, Georg (1990/1978 [1900/1907]). *The Philosophy of Money,* ed. David Frisby, trans. by Tom Bottomore and David Frisby. London and New York: Routledge.

Smelser, Neil, and Richard Swedberg, (Eds.) (1994). *The Handbook of Economic Sociology.* Princeton, NJ: Princeton University Press; and New York: Russell Sage Foundation.

Smith, Charles (1979). *A Critique of Sociological Reasoning.* Oxford: Basil Blackwell Publishers; and Totowa, NJ: Rowman and Littlefield.

——— (1981). *The Mind of the Market.* Totowa, NJ: Rowman and Littlefield.

——— (1982). "On the Sociology of the Mind." In *Explaining Human Behavior: Consciousness, Human Action, and Social Structure,* ed. Paul F. Secord. Beverly Hills, CA: Sage Publications.

——— (1989). *Auctions: The Social Construction of Value.* New York: Free Press (paperback edition [1990], Berkeley and Los Angeles: University of California Press).

Soros, George (1998). *The Crisis of Global Capitalism: Open Society Endangered.* New York: Public Affairs.

Sutherland, Edwin H. (1937). *The Professional Thief.* Princeton: NJ: Princeton University Press.

Swedberg, Richard (Ed.) (1990). *Economic and Sociology: Redefining Their Boundaries: Conversations with Economists and Sociologists.* Princeton, NJ: Princeton University Press.

———— ed. (1993). *Explorations in Economic Sociology.* New York: Russell Sage Foundation.

Thompson, Grahame, Jennifer Frances, Rosalind Levačić, and Jeremy Mitchell (eds.) (1991). *Markets, Hierarchies & Networks: The Coordination of Social Life.* London: Sage Publications.

Turner, Ralph H., and Lewis M. Killian (1957). *Collective Behavior.* Englewood Cliffs, NJ: Prentice-Hall.

Weber, Max (1947). *The Theory of Social and Economic Organization.* Trans. Talcott Parsons. New York: Free Press.

———— (1963). *The Sociology of Religion.* Boston: Beacon Press.

Whyte, William F. (1955). *Street Corner Society: The Social Structure of an Italian Slum.* Chicago, IL: University of Chicago Press.

Zelizer, Viviana A. (1994). *The Social Meaning of Money.* New York: Basic Books.

Zey, Mary (1993). *Banking on Fraud Drexel Junk Bonds and Buyouts.* New York: Aldine de Gruyter.

INDEX

(Glossary items are not automatically listed in this index. Cross referencing is, therefore, advised. Indexed items that appear in the Glossary are marked with an asterisk.)

ABOUT THE AUTHOR

CHARLES SMITH is professor and chair of Sociology at Queens College, CUNY. His earlier book, *The Mind of the Market,* was an Alternative Selection of the Book of the Month Club and Fortune Book Club.

332.6   Smith, Charles W.,
SMI   1938-

          Success and survival
          on Wall Street.

$22.95

DATE			

10116